If You Only Knew

LETTERS FROM AN IMMIGRANT TEACHER

Emily Francis

Published by Seidlitz Education
P.O. Box 166827
Irving, TX 75016
www.seidlitzeducation.com

For related titles and support materials visit www.seidlitzeducation.com.

8.22

Introduction

"My parents crossed the border so I could cross the stage."

During my first year teaching at Concord High School, one of my students wrote this on her graduation cap. This simple yet powerful way she expressed her appreciation for her parents' sacrifices hit me hard. It made me think about the enormous impact our personal journeys can make — not only on our own lives, but on the lives of the people we love.

The stories you are about to read are those of my own students. Their names have been changed to protect them as minors, but all parties were honored to have their stories shared. I hope the letters you find within these pages provide motivation, comfort, and inspiration for you on your own journey. But if you don't take anything else from this book, please just remember these two things:

First, you are not alone. No matter what obstacles you're facing, whether it's being new to a country or even just trying to fit in, we all struggle in some way at some point in our lives, and we often feel alone in those struggles. But let these letters remind you that there is always someone out there who's been through something similar...if you only knew their stories. If they survived — if they came out on the other side, braver and more confident than before — then so can you.

Second, tell your story. Our stories can help others find the strength to overcome their own difficulties, but only if we're willing to share them. Sharing and listening to each other's stories is the best way to build the kind of empathy that we all need in order to connect with each other. Other people's stories have supported and inspired me through some of the biggest moments in my life — some you'll read about here and some I've kept for myself.

You may not be ready to share everything just yet, and that's okay. To the extent that you can, I encourage you to tell your story. Talk to others about your experiences, and encourage your friends and family to share their experiences with you.

If this book inspires you to begin telling your story, you can start with me. Write me a letter or send me an email. I can't wait to learn more about each one of you.

Your teacher always,

Ms. Francis

Contents

chapter 1

Orlando

Dear Orlando,

When I first saw you in the classroom, I didn't see your ankle bracelet, but I'd heard about it. I had received an email before you arrived. It wasn't telling me to keep an eye on you but just letting me know that you were coming with an ankle bracelet because ICE had picked you up after you crossed the border. The bracelet wasn't the result of some horrible crime you'd committed; it was a souvenir of the time you'd spent in la hielera. As soon as I read that email, my heart broke for you. I could only imagine what you had been through just to get here. Because I had experienced some of the same things, I knew how difficult the journey had been, and I could imagine the fear you had felt in the moment you were caught. I also got caught entering the country undocumented, and I remember the feelings and thoughts that went through my mind. I remember that moment when I began to lose hope and to fear that the dreams I'd worked so hard for were just falling apart.

I could also imagine the fear you probably felt as you prepared to walk into a brand new school in a brand new country, so I made a promise that when you walked through that door into our school, I would make sure your experience would be a whole lot different than the one you had in that icebox with immigration.

On your first day of school, I noticed right away how put together you were. You had a cute little haircut, you were all cleaned up, and you wore a burgundy shirt and long black pants. I couldn't help thinking you were all dressed up for a brand-new opportunity. I remember doing the same thing when I got to the United States: choosing my best hand-me-down outfit for my first day of school. We both did this because we appreciated the opportunity and freedom we had to attend school. We knew that education would be our key to shift our narrative. We wouldn't forget what we'd left behind, but we were summoning the courage to face the future before us — with the help of our best outfits. Like I had done, you were leaving behind everything you had experienced, and now you were here, starting something new.

You knew it wouldn't be easy. You were scared, you were shaking, and you were pale. But you were here. I introduced myself and made sure you knew that I spoke your language and that you were allowed to speak your language to me, to anyone in the classroom, and to anyone at the school. I made sure you knew how to get from class to class. I made sure you had lunch. I made sure you knew how to get to the bus at the end of the day. Above all, the very first day you were at school, I made sure you did not experience judgment or fear, but that you experienced a place where you were welcomed and felt a sense of belonging.

This was all so important to me because, even though I didn't know the particulars of your story, I had some inkling of what you'd been through. You see, I came from Guatemala, and before I could come into New York, I had to spend several weeks in Mexico City with two of my sisters, waiting for our smuggler to get our "documents" together.

Some of that time was a lot of fun! We were in the heart of Mexico City. We often walked around Plaza de la

Constitución in the Zócalo, where we saw vendors selling their goodies and tourists taking pictures of all the beautiful, historic buildings. It was very similar to the heart of Guatemala City! The familiarity was comforting in some ways, but the first time I saw it, I felt homesick, wishing I was back in my home country.

But not everything felt familiar! I'll never forget the time we stopped at the mercado to order our very first authentic Mexican meal. We couldn't believe how spicy the food was! It was delicious, but it was hard for us to eat. We were used to adding a little bit of spice to our food, but not nearly that much! When we looked around, we saw plenty of other kids eating the same spicy food with no problem, and we didn't want to be wimps! My sisters and I looked at each other, and without saying a word, we knew we had to eat every bite.

It seems so silly now, but another thing I remember are the squirrels! My sisters and I had never seen squirrels in real life. The first time we saw one we were so excited that we chased it until it climbed a tree and disappeared. Somehow this little excitement made us feel closer to our final destination. Seeing something we had never seen before gave us the strength we needed to continue holding on to hope.

Still, holding on wasn't always easy. We didn't know how long we would be in Mexico or what would be waiting for us when we got to New York. Sometimes, we weren't even confident we'd wake up the next morning.

I remember one day in particular when I was walking down the streets of Mexico City, wondering, "Why am I going through this? Why am I here?" I had been in Mexico for weeks with my two sisters. I'd been separated from my other siblings for just as long, and it had been two years since I'd seen my mom. I'd left everything behind in Guatemala, and I didn't know if I would make it to the United States. I was having trouble holding onto hope. I remember finding myself at the base of a famous statue called the Ángel de la Independencia. It was so tall, so beautiful, and so bright. I didn't know the statue was famous, but its golden color made it look important, towering over that four-way intersection. It looked so free, like nothing could get in its way. I couldn't stop staring at it, wondering if I would ever feel that free — if all this time that felt so wasted and purposeless would ever be worth anything. Have you ever had that feeling, Orlando? When you're 15, it's almost impossible to think beyond what's happening at the moment. You can hardly imagine how your current circumstances could one day mean so much more than they do right now, but I promise you, they will. Whatever pain you experienced back home in El Salvador or on your journey into the United States, you'll be able to use it to do a whole lot of good one day.

That happened for me twenty-five years after I first stared up at the Ángel de la Independencia. I saw my experiences come full circle, and I finally understood their purpose. Our state, North Carolina, has an amazing program that takes teachers to different parts of the world every year to experience other cultures. I had been to Germany with the program once, and I'd gotten to know the directors a little bit. They knew I was an immigrant, that I spoke Spanish, and that I was capable of being a teacher leader in the program. So, they asked me to guide a group of 41 teachers through Mexico City to help them understand what it was like to be an immigrant and an undocumented traveler. Hopefully, this would help those teachers better understand their students' experiences and needs.

I agreed, and the itinerary they gave me included the same roads I'd walked and the same places I'd visited during my time in Mexico City as a 15-year-old immigrant. So there I was, 25 years later, standing once more beneath the Ángel de la Independencia. Only that time, I knew exactly what I was doing. I was sharing my immigrant story with 41 teachers, explaining what it felt like to be hungry and thirsty, to not know where you're going, but to hold onto hope so that you can start a new life when you get to the United States.

When I was 15 and finally started high school in New York, I still held onto hope. I was hoping for teachers who could understand my experiences, be patient, and highlight what was best in me (this is also why I made sure you had a path ready and waiting for you when you showed up at Concord High School; I wanted you to feel seen, heard, and validated). Many years later, there I was, 40 years old, helping those teachers become the kind of teachers my 15-year-old self so desperately craved — and the kind of teachers you and your fellow newcomers need.

Orlando, your experiences are important too. I know you have different hopes and dreams than I did, but the moments you may have considered a "waste of time in your life" can still shape you and become a foundation for your growth and success.

The first time I saw you, I didn't know how difficult your experiences were, and I wasn't sure how far to push and how much to ask without hurting you, but I wanted you to know that I cared about what you'd been through. So, I shared my story with you and your classmates, and we talked about other people — in our books and in the real world — who experienced the same things. You started opening up a little bit, which allowed me to get to know you enough to begin putting the puzzle together piece by piece.

When you showed me the video of you getting on that little boat to cross the Rio Grande into the United States, I saw just how strong you really are. My favorite part was how you held your mother's hand and helped her step onto the boat before you. Not only does that highlight what a gentleman you are, letting your mother go first, but it demonstrates that you're on her team, trusting her to do her best by you and having her back as you both take that step toward a better future. I knew you were scared from the look on your face and the way you moved so carefully and deliberately, but you did it anyway.

As I watched you take your own step onto the boat, I remembered the moment I stepped onto a bus to travel from Guatemala to Mexico. I felt both fear and a sense of purpose in that moment, and I imagine that you must have felt those things too. Those were steps of fear, steps into the unknown, but they were also steps of hope, steps of bravery, and steps toward what was best for us. Just like you, Orlando, I came in undocumented. We both knew what we were doing was technically wrong, but we were doing it to open doors we could not have opened at home. I also knew that for you, stepping on that boat was something you had to do for your own safety.

I know you were being recruited by gang members, and I can't understand or imagine the added fear of violence and the threats you received back home. I can only imagine what kind of proof your mother had to carry with her so that ICE would not force you to return to El Salvador. But one thing I can be sure of is that it doesn't matter how you got to this country, I know you're going to make the best of it now that you're here.

Part of making the best of it means finding your passions, using them to start building a new life for yourself, and showing others how vibrant and talented you are. When you first came into my classroom, I knew I needed to find what passion burned in your heart so I could highlight it for you and you could show others who you are before you even learned English. To this day, I wish I had been given opportunities to share my passions. I was so good at public speaking and giving presentations, but I was never given a chance to shine simply because I didn't speak English. Today, as an educator, I can think of hundreds of ways I could've shown what I was capable of. I could do critical thinking. I could learn what was being taught. I wasn't dumb, but I sure felt like I was, and I couldn't let the same thing happen to you. I *had* to find out what your passion was.

When I asked you what you love, what you used to do back home that you want to continue doing, your eyes lit up immediately. "Soccer," you said without hesitation. "I played soccer. I was good on the field." You even told me what position you played. I didn't really know what that meant, but all I needed to hear was soccer. Our school had a soccer team, so I quickly reached out to our coach and said, "I have a newcomer who does not speak English, but he is passionate about soccer."

I wasn't worried about you not fitting in because I knew the team had other English learners who could help you out, and I could tell by the way you talked about soccer that you would do just fine on the field.

Sure enough, you exceeded everybody's expectations—even your own, I think!

I know you were upset that I missed so many of your games because of my daughter's karate lessons, but you didn't need me to be your cheerleader. You were doing what you were good at, and you were thriving. Everybody kept telling me how good you were, and the soccer coach even texted me about you. He said, "You sent me a good one." This warmed my heart, and I knew I had done what I needed to do. I smiled, knowing that you were going to be just fine.

Then, right before your last game, you were nominated as the Charlotte Observer Athlete of the Week, and our whole class was so proud and so excited to support you. We knew you just had to win! Not only were you qualified, but you needed that victory and that platform and that chance to shine. So we all started voting for you and sharing the nominations, asking everyone we knew to vote for you too. We must have voted for you a hundred times each, and you even voted for yourself, too, remember?

You won, Orlando! We couldn't have been prouder. We put it on Facebook. We put it on Twitter and Instagram. We celebrated during class. We took pictures, and I made you a banner (which you took, by the way). I hope it's hanging in your room as a reminder of just how amazing you are. We celebrated even more when the Department of Education superintendent sent you a letter of congratulations. (I loved seeing that letter framed in your room during your video assignment long after the game!)

Do you remember when a big group of us got together to cheer you on in our last game that season? I knew you were good, and I knew you were happy, but watching you play, Orlando, was an incredible experience. You came to life on that field! You were—and you still are—a model for all of our students. You illustrated what it means to run full force into what you're passionate about and use it to show others who you really are.

I admire you so much, Orlando, because you embraced the challenges of coming to a new country. You didn't know what would happen, whether it would be hard or easy, and you didn't really understand the process. Still, you took the chance that it would work out for the best.

I admire the way you just go for it, then and now. You got on a boat, got in a car, got on a bus, and just held on to hope that what you are doing is going to transform your life. Everything you do, whether it's that first step on that boat, or walking down the street, or going in and out of smugglers' houses, has the potential to come back in life to help you reach your dreams.

Your teacher <u>always</u>,

Ms. Francis

chapter 2

Aida

Dear Aida,

You were so upset yesterday when you skipped lunch and showed up in my classroom. Your story just poured out of you. It broke my heart to see you hurting like that, but I was glad to be able to tell you that you weren't alone because I'd been in your shoes.

You seemed so different the first time I met you in Ms. Morgan's class. Do you remember it? When you stood up to talk with me, I found myself looking way up at you, embarrassed by how short I was. I couldn't tell where you were from. At first, I thought you might be Dominican because of your beautiful curly hair, but of course that assumption turned out to be wrong. Now I know you're of Mexican heritage. You weren't proficient in English yet (see how far you've come?), but you could read and write beautifully in Spanish. So when you transferred to my ESL class, we found ways for you to do the assignments in both languages while you were learning English. It was amazing to watch you set standards for yourself and then fight to meet (and often beat) them.

I knew you were here in the United States without your parents and that you missed them terribly. Still, in your first year here, you were so focused on your schoolwork that it seemed you hardly had time to think about that. You were so determined to show your parents that the sacrifice they had made was paying off. It was important to you to get the highest scores possible and make sure you were doing everything exactly right.

And then, when you found out your parents were sending your little sister, Cecilia, to the United States, you couldn't wait to have her with you! You bounced around the classroom, telling me all about her, and we counted down the days together until her arrival. I could tell that the idea of having Cecilia with you was, in some ways, the encouragement you needed to continue fighting the fight. I also knew you were looking forward to having a little piece of "back home" here with you.

But when Cecilia finally made it here (even though you were delighted to see her again), something began to

seem different about you. You'd been here on your own
for a year, but when your sister arrived, you suddenly
had to take on a role you hadn't expected: the role of her
mother. Now you had to take on the responsibility of
making sure Cecilia was eating, showering, and doing her
homework. I remember wondering if that responsibility
was perhaps taking away from your ability to take care of
yourself and your schoolwork.

Now that I know that's the case, I want to tell you my
story because I know how you feel. See, I was born and
raised in Guatemala, with four younger siblings. Like you
and Cecilia, I spent years living without my mom because
she left us to go to New York City when I was just thirteen years old. Even before that, though, I had always
been kind of like another parent to my little brother and
sisters. And, as you've learned, the "big sister duties" aren't
something we can read about in a manual or guidebook.
Instead, our duties and responsibilities as big sisters
come from our hearts; they're part of our cultures and
backgrounds. You're like me, Aida, in that you love and
embrace the role, and you do it as well as you can.

I loved having my mom with us when we lived in Guatemala, but even so, life was sometimes difficult. It must have been hard for her as a single mom with five kids, constantly working and trying to make enough money to take care of us. She never made enough money for us to buy our own house or car. It was always just enough to pay for rent and basic groceries: chicken legs, black beans, tortillas, and bread. And since my mom was working so hard to provide for us, my siblings often became my responsibility. As the oldest sister, my job was to help with the cooking, the cleaning, and the laundry. Oh, the stories I have of my cooking! My siblings had no choice but to eat what I had prepared, and on some days I'm sure they regretted it.

I learned to cook primarily by watching my mom and getting creative with what we could afford. When I went to the *mercado*, I'd always make sure I stretched the money so all six of us would be able to eat. We never had extravagant meals, but they were very filling. *Frijoles negros con arroz y tortillas* always did the trick.

My mother liked to have a clean home, so I'd make all

my siblings help me keep it that way. I tried to make it a game so it didn't feel like work, but laundry was always hard. We lived in places where we didn't have running water, and we had only seen washing machines in movies. We washed our clothes in a *pila* — a stand that held water in the middle and had countertops on each side. Then, we'd hang our clothes on a line to dry. But before we did any of that, we had to carry buckets of water from the factory nearby. To try to make it fun, I'd give each of my sisters a bucket, and we'd compete to see who could collect the most water.

I was also in charge of bathing all the kids, and I remember more than one time when my sisters got all dirty just after I had given them their baths and put them in clean clothes. They were always playing with mud, dirt, or anything else they could find to entertain themselves. But more important than keeping them from getting dirty or making sure they helped me with chores, my main goals were to keep them safe and make sure they got along — at least enough that they wouldn't kill each other! In a lot of ways, my childhood was fun, and we seemed just like other kids. We played with Barbie dolls. We played house.

We played tag. I even remember us constantly making up games to keep ourselves entertained, like I'm sure you and Cecilia have done hundreds of times.

But, unlike many kids, we also had to help our mother earn enough money to survive. My mom's business involved traveling three hours to the coast, where she would buy a truck full of the cheapest goods she could find — sometimes it was oranges or cauliflower or bundles of clothing from the United States called *pacas* — to bring back home so we could resell them at the market.

I did not enjoy working at our stand, but I knew I needed to help my family because we needed to buy milk and bread and pay our rent. When I worked at the market, I often saw other kids running around playing, or buying things instead of selling them, and I wondered what it would be like to be one of those kids.

I must have been about nine years old when my mother started this business. That's also when I learned how to drive. Often my mom asked my siblings and me to take the truck around town and knock on doors to help sell our goods faster so she could go back and get more. I liked the fact that my mother trusted me with such a big responsibility because it affirmed that I was doing my job well. But at the same time, it felt very intimidating to knock on doors and ask strangers to buy my oranges, or whatever I was selling that day. I think people purchased our stuff out of pity when they saw the kids and me begging. We gave them bargains, and we really played up how good our products were. At nine years old, I learned to be a little business manager, with a sales team that included my little sisters and brother.

But even working as hard as we did, we didn't always have enough money for a stable life. Unfortunately, we just lived in too many different places. If we couldn't sell enough of our products to afford the rent in one place, we would have to move to another, and then another and another. Since we were moving around so much, I was constantly changing schools. I don't think I ever spent a whole year in one school. Because of this, I never really had any friends. As soon as I would get used to a school and make some new friends, we would have to move again, and I would have to start at another school. It was difficult for me, and I know it was hard for my sisters too.

I don't know how the schedule worked for your school in Mexico, but in Guatemala, our schools had two different shifts. We could go in the morning or the afternoon, and I would choose based on when I needed to be working in my mom's business or taking care of my siblings. Often, I was too busy at home to go to either shift. The schools always seemed really far away too. I remember having to walk two hours to get to one school when I was in fifth grade. My eldest sister, Leslie, and I walked together. We had to wake up super early to get ready, but our trips were fun. Sometimes we would stop at the store and buy a snack that we would share on the way. Unfortunately, that year school was just too far to walk, and it felt like a waste of time when I knew I could be providing for my family instead. I failed that grade and had to repeat it. Don't get me wrong! It's not that I didn't like school or appreciate education — I did! But that year, surviving and supporting my family were higher priorities than going to school.

That's what it was like when my mom was around. She took good care of us, but I had to step in and help with my brother and sisters a lot just so we could survive in Guatemala. But once she went to New York and we were on our own, I really did become my siblings' "mom." The way I saw it, they needed a mom, so they had me!

My point is that I know what it's like to be an "unaccompanied minor" playing mom to my own siblings. Sometimes I still feel like I'm everybody's mom.

I don't know what prompted your parents to send you and Cecilia here to the United States, but for my family, it took some extremely tough circumstances to get my mom to make that difficult choice.

Everything began spiraling downward for us after she started dating this nightclub owner named Oscar. In the beginning, Oscar seemed okay. He helped us out with the rent, which was nice, but he also started taking my mom to his bar and other places where she was exposed to many of the drugs that were so prevalent in that scene. Eventually, he and my mom split up, but she'd become addicted by then, and her business began to collapse. She would even use drugs right in front of me and the kids. I begged her to stop. We needed to continue our business, and we couldn't do it without her, but I just couldn't seem to get through to her. When she wasn't using, she was out looking for more or passed out at home.

When she was out of commission, it fell entirely to me to take care of the kids, now with less money than ever before. Even making dinner for all of us sometimes seemed impossible. I remember having just enough money to make chicken feet soup one day — not even chicken, just chicken feet. The feet were all I could afford. But I made soup out of those chicken feet, and after I served the kids, I tried to wake mom up. I remember saying, "Mommy, wake up, have some soup." I wanted her to wake up so badly. No, I didn't just want her to wake up — I needed her to wake up. I needed her to be with us. I *needed* her to go buy more oranges so we could get back to the business.

When she finally woke up, I could tell she wasn't really with us. I convinced her to eat some soup, but she just walked out the door as soon as she was finished. She was in really bad shape when she left, and I began to fear that she wouldn't ever come back. I worried about what to do with all the kids, especially my youngest brother, who was only three or four months old at the time. We had no idea where she went, and the longer she was gone, the more convinced I became that the kids and I were on our own. Fortunately, my mom did come back the following day. It's a moment I will never forget. When she burst through the door, she seemed like a whole different person. For a second, I thought my soup must have been magic or something. She was shouting, *"Conocí al Señor! Conocí al Señor!"* and I started getting really nervous. Oh, no! I thought. She met another guy? What are we in for now?

But then she explained what happened to her. She told us that she had been walking down the street, feeling lost and depressed, certain that she was going to die. She was sobbing uncontrollably because she wanted to be a better mom for us. She just wanted to get cleaned up. While she was wandering, she came across this church called El Calvario and decided to go in. There was a young woman inside cleaning, and she turned out to be the pastor's daughter. When she saw my mom crying, she asked if she could pray for her. My mom tried to describe what happened next, telling us that when the young woman began praying for her, she felt something "happen" inside. She said she felt "instantly cleansed." We slowly began to realize what had happened to my mom. She hadn't met just any old *señor*. She'd met *el Señor* — the Lord.

Aida, I know this may sound too good to be true, but my
mom acted so differently from that point on. She stopped
drinking and stayed sober. She started to seem more
conscientious about everything she was doing and became
determined to do what was best for us. She became laser-
focused on the business, and I was able to go to school
a little more often and finally pass the fifth grade. Still,
our problems didn't magically disappear. She had stopped
using drugs, but that also meant she no longer hung
around the kind of people who could help her get easy
cash. While we were all so grateful for her transformation
and her health, the business of selling oranges just didn't
provide enough to pay the bills.

Our breaking point came one night when I was thirteen.
We had made *frijoles con arroz* for dinner, but we only
had enough for my two youngest siblings. That night, as
we sat there watching them eat while the rest of us went
without, my mom decided she had to go to the United
States to see if she could provide a better future for us.

She'd been sober for two years by that point and made
the decision with a clear mind. She said she would make
a way for us — to give us a better future, a better house,

and more food — and I knew she meant it. Eventually, my siblings and I would make our way to the United States on our own, but until we got there, it would be my responsibility to take care of them in our mom's place.

Of course I had heard stories about people leaving Guatemala for the United States, making blended families, and forgetting about the people they left behind. Friends also used to tell me, "That's it! Your mom is gone, and she'll never return. She'll stop sending money little by little until she forgets about you." They didn't say this to be mean; they said this because it happened in our town all the time. You'd hear kids sharing their stories of how their loved ones had promised so much and then just disappeared. There was a part of me that would fill with doubt whenever I heard those stories, but I had to be strong and reassure my siblings that this was not going to be the case for us. One way or another, we would one day be together again. And besides, I trusted my mom completely; I'd seen how she'd changed. I knew she was going to pack her bags and head to the United States. I knew that as soon as she arrived she was going to start sending money and she was going to make a better future for us. She had proven now that she wanted to and that she could. I think about those stories when I see some of Cecilia's pictures on Instagram of her and her friends back in Mexico, with captions about how much she misses the people she left behind. My heart breaks for her when I see those. I know you want her to focus on her studies, but I wonder if staying in touch with her boyfriend and her other friends is helping her feel less lonely while she copes with her own challenges here in the United States.

When my mom left, she split us up so we could all have someone taking care of us. The younger ones (Lizbeth, Gabriela, and Abner) went to stay with one of my mom's friends. My oldest sister, Leslie, and I were supposed to stay with a neighbor, but the neighbor backed out. That's how Leslie and I ended up having to stay with my dad and his wife.

My dad wasn't anybody's first choice. He had always been around, but he'd never been a resource for us. I hadn't even met him until my mother was planning her trip to the United States. She told him she was leaving and his daughters — Leslie and me — would stay behind because he needed to be aware that we were on our own in case we needed something. So, he agreed to meet us for the first time. I was nervous, but I was looking forward to finally meeting the man who gave me my existence. Unfortunately, when we arrived at his house, he was knocked out drunk. He wanted to hug me and say hello, but I just remember being overwhelmed by his stink. I was so disappointed. I almost wished I'd never met him.

Leslie and I moved in with him after my mom left, and the situation quickly deteriorated when my stepmother began verbally abusing us. I also learned that Lizbeth, Gabriela, and Abner were being physically abused by the people who were supposed to be taking care of them. So I called my mom and told her I needed to get all the kids back together. A friend from church agreed to let us build a shack in his backyard and keep an eye on us. All five of us could live together there, with me taking care of all the kids.

Leslie, Lizbeth, and Gabriela were old enough to understand what was going on, at least a little, but my little brother, Abner, was too young to remember what life was like before our mom left. I was the only mother figure he knew, and I took the role seriously. I remember feeding him, bathing him, playing with him — doing whatever I thought a mother would do.

But when Abner was three years old, he began doing something that really terrified me: he started calling me "Mom." I was only thirteen — I wasn't old enough to be somebody's mother! Sure, it was common to see a very young girl becoming a mother in our town. Take my own mother, for example: she was only sixteen when she had me. By the age of twenty-five, she already had five children. But I saw those young mothers — girls my age or just a little older — having to stay home to do chores and take care of their kids. It was definitely not what I envisioned for my life, especially after my own "motherhood" experience of taking care of four siblings. I still had so much to learn about taking care of myself! And yet, here I was, taking care of my little brother and my three other siblings as if they were my own children. As I fully took on this role, something began happening to me inside. I started believing that I had to make my entire life about them. I poured everything I had into them. Everything.

Aida, I sometimes fear the same thing might be happening to you in your relationship with Cecilia. Believe me, I understand the weight you feel on your shoulders. You feel the need to honor your parents by caring for your sister. You feel like you need to be your parents in their absence, and you feel like you'll fail them if you don't do your part. But I fear that, in doing all that, you could lose sight of what you need to be doing for yourself.

I wasn't fully able to start shifting away from the "mommy" role until after we came to the United States. Of course, I still helped take care of Abner and the others, but my responsibilities shifted. I would keep an eye on them while my mom was working, and I would still make them dinner once in a while, but they didn't need me to be their mom anymore, so I got to be their big sister again.

The process of "letting go" wasn't easy, but once I was in the United States, I had to start focusing on myself. I had to go to school — I *wanted* to go to school — and I had to be successful to reach my own dreams.

I know our experiences aren't identical, but I think it's time for you to start doing the same. I think maybe Cecilia doesn't really need you to be her mom right now either. In fact, just like you, she is probably eager to have her sister back because she's lonely without you. (Don't tell her I said that! She so desperately wants to be strong!)

I know it can be easy to resent your parents for asking you to navigate this balance between mother and sister, but one thing I've learned is that our parents pay a huge price when they decide to be so far away from us. They sacrifice so much out of love for us, and I know they don't take it lightly. I received my sixth-grade diploma after my mom left Guatemala for the United States. It was my first graduation ceremony, and my mother wasn't there. It was a difficult time for me, but looking back, I realize it was even more difficult for my mother. She missed a huge milestone her firstborn had achieved, and she wasn't able to enjoy the fruit of her hard work. But the reason she missed my sixth-grade graduation — and other milestones too — was that she loved her children so much that she was willing to sacrifice to secure a better future for us. Believe me when I say it's okay to feel angry, but keep in mind that this separation is so, so hard for your parents too.

Just remember that the role you're playing right now is temporary, and it's already changing. You might try shifting from thinking of it as the burden of being Cecilia's "mother" to thinking of it as an opportunity to be her helpful big sister. Ensure that she has food and that she's safe, and encourage her when she needs it, but don't feel obligated to watch her every move and guide her through every decision. She is old enough to take care of her own success while you take care of yours.

I can see how strong, intelligent, and driven you are, and I want to see you give yourself the time and energy to embrace those things in order to thrive as a young adult. Even though you grew up in Mexico, you have an advantage by having been born here in the United States. Your citizenship can help you in so many ways — getting a driver's license, going to college, and getting a job, for starters — but you have to be successful in school for any of that to matter.

Do you remember that afternoon, earlier this semester, when you threw your papers across the classroom? You were so angry with yourself. You were struggling with the assignment, and you had this picture in your mind of what your best work would look like, but you just couldn't figure out how to bring it to life. You were ready to throw in the towel. But do you remember why you were struggling so much? It was because you'd set out to do even more than I'd asked. Your assignment was to write a single sentence in English, but you'd decided to write a whole paragraph instead, just like your native English-speaking classmates. It was difficult, and you got frustrated, and that's why you threw your papers across the room. I was afraid for a moment that you really were giving up, but I felt so elated when I saw you take out another piece of paper and start working again. You set the bar so high for yourself, and you wrote that whole paragraph that day. You were so proud!

At that moment, all I could think was how I wished your parents could see the responsible and brave young lady you're becoming. I had the privilege of watching you grow the way a mother watches her own children grow every single day. I would have given anything at that moment to have had your parents experience the joy I was experiencing just by watching you.

You're dealing with a lot right now, but I've seen what you can handle, and I've seen what your sister can handle. So throw those papers as often as you need — just keep taking out fresh ones and trying again. You deserve it.

I know sometimes you aren't sure if you do. I know you feel like Cecilia has to come first all the time right now, and that makes you a wonderful sister, but you deserve to focus on yourself too. Cecilia's old enough to take care of herself and to make many decisions for herself. If she fails, she's mature enough to take responsibility. I wouldn't tell you to start letting go if your sister was two or three years old, but she's old enough to do it on her own, and I believe you need to start taking care of yourself again now.

Believe me, I know playing mom can be so hard. You might be mad about it right now, you might be sad about it right now, and you might cry about it right now. That's okay. My sisters and I definitely did our fair share of crying and being mad back then, but we can all laugh about it today.

"Remember when you dropped a whole pot of soup on the floor?"

"Remember when you stuck me in the bathtub, clothes and all, because I'd had an accident?"

"Remember when you served us cold food because we were too hungry to wait until it was warm?"

"Remember when…?"

All those "remember whens" that we cried about in the moment still bring tears to our faces — but now they're tears of laughter. Those experiences created such a strong bond because we were working together to make life as good as we could possibly make it for ourselves. Now, as an adult, I look back and sometimes wish I had done things differently, but do you know what, Aida? I did the best I could, so now we just laugh. And now you're doing the best you can, and believe me, you and Cecilia will laugh one day too.

Your teacher *always*,

Ms. Francis

chapter 3

Cecilia

Dear Cecilia,

I spoke with Aida yesterday during lunch, and I learned
a little bit about how you two are having a hard time
getting along. I hope you don't feel like we were talking
about you behind your back, but when I saw how sad
and angry you both looked getting off the bus yesterday
morning, I could sense something was going on between
you two. (Since I have three sisters, I'm pretty good
at recognizing when sisters are fighting.) When Aida
stopped by my classroom during her lunch period, I had
to ask what was going on. I wanted to see if there was
anything I could do to help. After all, I wanted you both
to know that, even though your parents aren't close by, I'm
here and I care for you.

She told me you two were fighting about the time you're
spending on Facebook and Instagram, looking through
pictures and sharing stories of your friends from back in
Mexico. I know it's not fun for either of you when Aida

gets angry like that, but I hope you know she's worried about you. She knows what it takes to keep up with school while learning English at the same time because she struggles with it too, and she's afraid you're spending too much time missing your friends instead of concentrating on your schoolwork. She's upset because she feels like you're her responsibility, and she's afraid she's letting you and your parents down.

While Aida's right about making plenty of time for school, I can tell from your classwork that you're nowhere near falling behind. So I really hope you'll talk with your sister about how important it is for you to stay connected to your old friends, because those connections are a big part of your life! I know because I've seen some of your posts on Instagram. I've seen you put up old pictures of your school friends in matching uniforms, of you and your best friend Maria, and of you and your boyfriend in Mexico. I've read the captions you write, letting them know how much you miss them. (I've even seen you write some of those captions in English, and while my heart breaks for you, I'm proud to see you practicing your English like that!) I've even seen you making Snapchats to send to your parents!

I also know how important those connections are because I've been in your position. My mom came to the United States when I was thirteen, while my siblings and I stayed behind in Guatemala. When we were separated, I missed her so much. I think what I missed the most were those little moments we had together, whether we were cooking or spending time with all my siblings. We used to play tag in the backyard, all of us, and I remember on hot days, sometimes Mom would fill up buckets of water and chase us around with them, pouring them over our heads to cool us down. There were times she would sit with us in the evenings and tell us stories about things that had happened to her on the road as she drove to and from the coast. One time, she even told us how she thought she'd seen a ghost while she was driving! Those moments were what I missed the most while we were apart. I missed just having her there with me to do all those random, unimportant things we used to do. I imagine those are the kinds of things you miss about your friends and family as well.

When my mom was gone, I took on a lot of responsibility as an older sister. I took care of my siblings, making sure the older ones went to school and the younger ones were safe during the day. I went to school myself, as much as I could, and I managed the shopping, the cooking, the cleaning, and everything else. But despite all the work I had to do, no matter how busy I was, I always stayed connected with my mom by writing letters. We didn't have Facebook or Instagram back then (I know, I'm so old, right?), and phone calls were just too expensive. We could borrow a family friend's phone and call her in an emergency or for something really important, but long-distance calls could cost almost $300 per month. Though my mom could technically afford it, she had to prioritize how to spend the money she was making. She wanted to save as much as possible for us. Phone calls were just too expensive, but letters were really cheap to send. We used thin, lightweight paper, and we'd write long, long letters and fold them up as small as we could to tuck them into an envelope. We used these letters to tell my mom what we'd been doing.

We'd share funny stories, tell her about what we'd been cooking every night, and let her know if there was anything we needed (or anything we wanted — and that list sometimes got long!). Some letters were also full of *quejas*! My sister complained about how I made them work at home. I complained that my sisters wouldn't listen to me, and my little brother complained about not getting the remote control car he wanted. Most importantly, we used the letters to tell her how much we missed her and loved her. We'd draw hearts and make lipstick kisses on the pages for her. My two oldest sisters and I wrote our own letters, but the two little ones couldn't write yet. Instead, we would give them a piece of paper and have them scribble and doodle what they wanted to say, and we would "translate" what the doodles meant. "Tell Mommy this," they'd say, and, "Tell Mama that!" It was important for the little ones to feel heard and seen even if they couldn't write yet.

My mom would always write us back, and we carried on a yearslong conversation that way, with each letter a response to the one before. We kept all of the letters we wrote each other during those years — there must be hundreds — and I treasure them more than anything.

One time, I had this little clown sticker that I stuck on the letter I was writing to Mom. I drew a big speech bubble and wrote my message inside it like the clown was talking to her. I vividly remember looking at the clown and telling him, "Tell mom how we're doing!" I ran my fingers over it and placed it against my heart because I knew my mom would do the same. Sure enough, she took the clown from my letter and attached it to her own, with her message in another speech bubble. That little clown went back and forth from the United States to Guatemala for a long time!

Another time, my mom asked me to trace my feet and mail her the drawing so she could be sure to buy the right-sized shoes to send me. So I traced my foot, and then I put a sticker of two footprints on the same page, and I wrote a note telling her not to confuse those footprints with my real footprints. It was so silly, but being able to joke with Mom even when she was thousands of miles away made me feel so much closer to her.

A lot of our letters were silly and fun like that, though sometimes they were more serious. I remember one time, after my mom had been away from us about a year, she was really sad, really missing us, and she had told me on one of those very expensive phone calls that she was thinking about coming home. I told her I didn't think she should do that yet, and she took it the wrong way. She thought us kids didn't want her back, when the truth was that we wanted her back more than anything! I wrote her a letter explaining what I meant: that we missed her so much, but what would we do if she came back to Guatemala now? Sure, she'd have enough money to buy us a house, but then what? We'd go back to selling oranges at the market, and before we knew it, we'd be struggling just like before. I told her I wanted her to take advantage of the work she had in the United States. There I was, 14 or 15 years old, telling my mom to keep her head up, to keep trusting God, and that we were going to be prosperous and we were going to be together. We didn't know the details — my siblings and I hadn't even thought about going to the United States yet — but I was confident that everything was going to work out. I wanted my mom to be confident too. I wanted her to be strong and to keep her head up.

When she wrote me back, she said my letter had made her realize that the kids and I were okay and that, if we were going to change our lives for the better, she needed to keep working in the United States. Here's a little snippet of what she wrote to me:

"After we spoke by telephone, I was even sadder, wondering why you weren't as excited as I had hoped [about me coming home]. But you've given me a lot of answers, and I'm recalling what you asked about where I would work when I returned. Your words have made me think differently, and I think I'm being selfish not wanting to continue a little longer, to make something better for you all, who are all I have. Thinking about it, if I come back, I can buy us a little land and a house, but what would we live on? You and your siblings need studies, not just a roof...If you think you are well and happy and that you can wait a little longer, I will do everything in my power to stay here a while longer as long as, thanks to God, you and the little ones are well and I have good work."

Would you believe that a year after that letter was written, my sisters and brother and I were reunited with our mom in the United States? When I look back at letters like that, it almost makes me glad we didn't have Facebook, Instagram, or Snapchat. Sure, we would've communicated more frequently like you do with your friends and family, but I think seeing photos of our little shack — or of how skinny we'd all gotten — would've broken my mom's heart and made it even harder for her to stay in the United States. Even though we really were doing just fine with what we could afford, she wanted so much more for us. Fortunately, writing letters helped us have deeper and more meaningful conversations about what was really best for the family. At that point in our separation, she was on the brink of giving up and coming back home, but because we had worked so hard to stay connected, we were able to give each other the strength to be patient and make the tough decisions that would be so much better in the long run.

Before Mom left Guatemala, she promised that her reason for leaving us and coming to the United States was to work, send money, and give us a better future. In a way, my letters were a way I could encourage her to keep her promise, though it wasn't just me encouraging Mom. My little sister Gabriela pitched in too, drawing picture after picture of the house she imagined we would one day live in, with a pretty garden and everything. The night she told us she was leaving Guatemala, Mom had promised to one day build us a house like that, and Gabriela wasn't about to let her forget it!

Regularly hearing from Mom helped ease the fears that would come up when I saw other people whose families left for the United States and then forgot about them. I wanted to make sure that didn't happen to us, and writing letters was a way to ensure she knew we were still there, that we still needed her. A letter back meant she was still thinking about us. She'd tell us about walking the streets of Queens, New York, and seeing children having fun with their parents. When she saw kids who looked like us, she said she'd cry in desperation about not being able to hold her children close to her.

To feel closer to us, she would sometimes record herself talking to us and send us the cassette tapes so we could hear her voice. Even as far away as we were from the United States, we knew she was still right there with us.

Whether it's a letter like my siblings and I wrote to our mom or one of the posts you've tagged your friends in on Facebook, these connections are meant to keep our relationships strong, Cecilia. I know that you're maintaining these relationships, in part, as a way to cope with everything new and different and challenging — I know because that's what I did with my letters to my mom too. Maybe they feel like they're not that important, or like they're taking up energy that you should be spending on other things, but just look at how powerful all those letters we wrote back and forth turned out to be! One single letter kept us strong enough for another year of separation, and in the same way, every single post you make gives you the strength to thrive here in the United States, knowing that you have these strong relationships with friends who love you and who are rooting for you.

I know it might be tempting to shut off your phone and put your nose in your books just to please Aida and make it easier at home, but that would be so detrimental to you, Cecilia! I know that from experience. When I was a teenager in the United States, I went through some difficult times and shut off my connections. I didn't want to talk to anybody or be friends with anybody — I even left home! But if I had worked harder to stay connected with the people I love during that time, like I did during the years we were separated from our mom, I think it wouldn't have been quite as hard. Those relationships would've made me feel stronger.

I know the reason you're on social media so much is that you're looking for ways to stay connected, just like I did when my mom came to the United States. I also wrote Aida a letter, but I encourage you to talk to her as well. Tell her why your Instagram and Facebook posts are so important to you. Talk to her about how you're balancing your friends and your homework. Once she understands that you aren't just slacking or procrastinating, I bet she'll start to worry less.

You're doing the right thing, Cecilia, keeping up with your friends and family. Your dad called me just the other day, and we chatted about how you and Aida are doing in school and how the family is treating you here in the United States. He told me how glad he is to have social media as a way to stay connected with you since he's missing you back home. So don't overlook your schoolwork, but don't give up your Instagram either. And if you ever feel inspired, you might even try writing some old-fashioned letters!

Remember, I'm always here for both you and Aida. Anytime you want to rant or cry or talk about what you're missing, you know where to find me.

Your teacher **always**,

Ms. Francis

chapter 4

Mónica

Dear Mónica,

I just sat in on your math class, and I think I finally understand why you are struggling so much. It's not just that the math is hard or that you are struggling with English; it's also how you relate with Ms. Parks in the classroom. I'm impressed with how hard you're working, and I can see that you're great with numbers, but now that I know you so well, I know that you are more than capable of making things better for yourself in that class.

Before I met you, all I knew about you were your test scores. I knew that you did not score very well on your placement exam, and based on those numbers, I knew that you hadn't learned English in your home country. I had some sense of what you could and could not do in the classroom, and I knew you would need my support. Still, that was all just data. I didn't know you yet. I didn't know anything about your family, your experiences, or what you were like, but I couldn't wait to meet you.

The first time that I saw you, I couldn't figure out what country you were from. I even wondered for a moment if you were Egyptian, even though I knew you spoke Spanish. The first time I heard you speak, I couldn't place your beautiful accent. Your skin color is different from mine, and I love that about you. Your eye shape is different, too, and your hair is jet black. (I've never asked, but I suspect you dye it. It's beautiful, but it looks too dark to be natural.) So, after I introduced myself to you, the first thing I asked was where you're from. "Honduras," you said very quietly. I could tell from just this basic interaction that you were nervous and shy, and I knew that I wanted to get to know you more.

Well, I know so much more about you now, and I've loved every minute of working with you and getting to know you. I know you're smart and sweet, and I know you're working hard to take more risks in your classes, even though sometimes it's difficult.

I know you live with your mother and her partner, though you don't talk much about them or their relationship. I also know a little about some challenging experiences you've had that you don't want to share with your classmates. It sometimes breaks you when you think about it. I know it makes you cry sometimes, and you don't want to talk about it. I respect that. I've also had experiences I haven't told anybody about — not even my mother. I know what it's like to want to keep some memories hidden. I'm always here to listen, but I won't ever push you to share more than you want.

Most importantly, Mónica, I know you're a fighter.

I know because I've watched you fight. You get a tissue, and dry your tears, then you pull yourself back together and keep reading, keep working on your assignments. That's what a fighter does. I know because that's what I did. Fighters like us, we think about our experiences, and how they've broken us, but we don't give up. We use that broken energy to keep on with life, to climb up, to survive.

You are a fighter, Mónica, and even though you are shy sometimes, I know I can push you in ways I can't push every other student.

Do you remember the first time I pushed you? I'd been

working with you in your English 1 class for almost a
whole semester, and one day, when you came up to me
and asked, "*¿Puedo ir al baño?*" I told you it wasn't up
to me. If you wanted to use the restroom, you had to
ask your English teacher, and you needed to ask him in
English. You were scared, but I knew you could do it, so I
practiced with you — "May I please go to the bathroom?"
— and then sent you up to his desk. You were shaking,
but you did it perfectly.

And now look how far you've come! You hardly talk to
me in class at all! You know how to ask for just about
anything you need on your own. I see you asking for your
Chromebook. I see you asking to go to the bathroom. I
see you raising your hand and tapping the teacher on the
shoulder when you have a question. Half the time, I'm
the one who needs help understanding what's going on
with you! But that's exactly how it should be. It makes
me feel so satisfied knowing that you are taking matters
into your own hands and that you don't need me as much
anymore. When I started school in the United States, I
wasn't encouraged to take risks like that. Looking back,
I wish I'd had somebody pushing me — encouraging me
to ask to go to the bathroom in English, to stand up for

myself when it felt too hard. Not being able to speak for myself or interact in class just made me feel so inferior and worthless.

I enrolled in Martin Van Buren High School in Queens the day after I arrived in New York from Guatemala. It was just a bus ride away from our house. I had never seen such a beautiful campus and I was so excited. The building was clean, and when we walked in, the receptionist was dressed so nicely. It was a completely different environment from the schools I'd been to in Guatemala. And the best part was that, for the first time, I would finally get to put school first! I loved school, but I had always had to put our family business first at home, often working in the market instead of going to my classes. I would still have to work in the United States, and I'd still have to help my siblings with their homework, but for the first time I was going to get to prioritize my education. It was so exciting to walk into the school knowing that my most important job was learning!

Of course, I was scared too. Since I was fifteen years old already, I skipped straight from sixth grade to high school even though I didn't even speak as much English as you did when you first started. In fact, I had no background in English at all. I sometimes saw my friends chatting in groups and laughing, and I envied their ability to interact in both Spanish and English. I saw how easy it was for them to switch from one language to the other, and I longed to have the same ability. I also longed to interact with them the same way they interacted with each other and with our teachers.

Like you, I started figuring it out. I looked for people who could be mediators like I have been for you. Other students or teachers who spoke Spanish answered simple questions like where to get my tickets for lunch or my pass for the bus. But unfortunately, sometimes my mediators weren't as helpful as I hoped, and that led to plenty of frustrating and embarrassing moments. I especially struggled in my math class because I simply couldn't understand what my teacher asked from me. One day I knew he wanted some kind of work or assignment from me, but I didn't know what it was or how to do it. So I asked my friends, my mediators, how to tell him I didn't understand. My friends gave me the sentence, "I know nothing." I should have asked them what that really meant, but I trusted that they were helping me, giving me something useful to say like, "I can't understand the instructions," or maybe, "I don't speak English." I practiced my new sentence until I felt confident with it, and the next time the teacher asked me for an assignment, I looked him in the eye and said, "I know nothing."

I hoped the teacher would respond by helping me understand what he was asking, but instead of lifting the burden off my shoulder, he turned around and made fun of me, making everyone laugh by making me feel like I was stupid.

He wrote on the board, "1 + 1 = 2" and then he turned and looked at me. "You know nothing?" he asked, pointing to the ridiculous equation. Of course I knew one plus one equals two. What I wished I knew was how to tell him I wasn't stupid. I just didn't understand the assignment he was asking me to complete.

I was so humiliated. Even looking back on it now, it's hard to remember that time without feeling small and embarrassed and angry.

When you came into my classroom to tell me you were

having trouble understanding Ms. Parks, I saw that same burden on your shoulders. I wanted to do whatever I could to lift it the way my math teacher should have done for me. When I started coming to your class to find out why you're having a hard time, I saw immediately that it wasn't your fault. You knew the math. When I explained it to you in Spanish, it was no problem for you. You just don't understand the English explanations yet, and Ms. Parks doesn't know how to help. She speaks too fast, she doesn't turn toward you when she's talking to you, and she doesn't come and check your work. She doesn't go above and beyond to make sure that you're understanding.

As I see it, you have two options: you can blame Ms. Parks and continue to struggle in math without her help, or you can channel your frustration and take matters into your own hands like I've watched you do in your English class. After my math teacher made me feel so awful, I decided to take control of my own learning. I went home and got a bunch of dictionaries and thesauruses, and I started translating all of my assignments into Spanish so I could do the work. It took much longer that way — hours and hours. In fact, my mother would often wake up past midnight to find me at the kitchen table, either doing my work or asleep on my notebook after a long night of studying. But it was worth it because it kept me from falling behind in my classes. As my English improved, I didn't have to do that as much, but until then, translating everything allowed me to keep up with the content. I was determined to never again feel like I "knew nothing."

My negative experience not only encouraged me to fight and stand up for myself, but to find ways to prove to myself and my teachers that I could do it.

Mónica, don't hold Ms. Parks accountable for your learning. Instead, take charge, and show her that you can learn. Make a list of specific things you can do to help yourself understand things better in her class. Your list might include having a conversation with her. Let her know what she's doing that is working for you and what isn't. You might be surprised at how she responds. Just remember that being a fighter doesn't always mean fighting alone. I can help you prepare for that conversation if you want.

Even once your English is perfect, you'll still encounter things you don't understand. That's just an unfortunate part of life. And there will be people — coworkers, bosses, acquaintances — who don't want to help you or don't know how to help you. The more you practice standing up for yourself now, the easier it will be with every obstacle you encounter in the future.

I know doing this is hard, Mónica, but you've already shown me and everyone else that you are capable of doing hard things. Remember, I'm here for you if you need anything.

Your teacher always,
⁚ὥ⁚ Ms. Francis

chapter 5

Raquel

Dear Raquel,

Mrs. Barnes texted me that you were in some kind of trouble and asked if I could check on you since you and I have a closer relationship than you have with her. I wasn't sure exactly what kind of trouble you were in, but when you came into my classroom, I could see the panic in your eyes from miles away. It was the same panic I'd seen the day I met you.

That first day we met, I walked into the English 2 class and did a quick scan of the room, trying to guess which student I was supposed to help. When I first saw you, I assumed it wasn't you because you had an attitude that clearly said you didn't need any help from anybody. You looked at me, looked away, and rolled your eyes, clearly saying, "I don't know who you are, and I don't care." You were also very well dressed. You had your makeup and hair done all cute, and you had on these fancy little *chancletas* with feathers on them. I have to admit, I wondered why you would wear those flip-flops to school instead of something more practical, but then again, it was my first year teaching high school, so I wondered about a lot of things.

Anyway, I was pretty sure you weren't my student, but when I saw the name tag on your desk, I realized that you were. I knew I would have to get past your eye rolls and your attitude to see if I could get to know you. So I went to your desk, got down on your level, and introduced myself. I knew you'd been in the United States for a year and a half, so I started with English. "Hi, my name is Ms. Francis, I am your ESL teacher, and I am here to help you."

That's when I saw the panic in your eyes for the first time. I recognized that panic because I've felt it myself, many times — even as an adult. It's the specific panic that comes when someone asks something you don't understand and you fear you'll be made fun of for not understanding, or that all they'll see is your inability to speak English instead of everything you're really capable of. This panic is so real and so strong that it makes us protect ourselves from anyone who might harm us. We prefer to isolate rather than risk being hurt. We prefer either working extra hard or giving up altogether rather than letting others see our weaknesses. When I was in high school, I didn't have an ESL teacher coming to see me in my core courses like you do. I often felt I had to isolate myself from my peers so they wouldn't notice that I felt different and mock me or look down on me. So I get you, Raquel, and believe me, there's nothing wrong with coping this way.

Still, when I realized you hadn't understood a word of what I'd said, I wondered how you had made it through a year and a half without learning to understand even the most basic introduction. I'd worked with enough students to know that after that long, you should have been able to understand me, even if you weren't comfortable speaking or writing yet. That was a big red flag for me, so I looked into your records and realized that you hadn't received any direct instruction to help you acquire English the entire time you'd been in the United States. No wonder you were panicked! No wonder you'd put up such a big wall! So, I decided to help you. I started by asking the school to move you to my newcomer class so we could give you the foundation you'd missed.

In the meantime, I tried my introduction again, this time

in Spanish. *"Hola, me llamo Sra. Francis. Soy tu maestra de inglés como segunda lengua, y te voy a ayudar."* And at that moment, the panic in your face changed to relief, and though you didn't let that wall down yet, you nodded your head. *"Estoy aquí para ayudarte,"* I said. *"Si necesitas algo, dime."* And you just said, "Okay," and looked away.

"Estoy aquí para ayudarte." Oh, how I wish someone would've said these words to me when I was in school. On many occasions, I felt like I was drowning. I felt lost and so impotent. It infuriated me, and it killed me because I knew I was capable of everything school asked of me — I just couldn't do it in English yet. I always longed for a teacher to approach me in my struggles and help me out. Like you, I wasn't looking for someone to do the work for me or to make it easier. I just longed for the opportunity to demonstrate my full potential, but I was too afraid that my teachers assumed I was lazy or stupid for not doing my job or completing my assignments. And so, just like you, instead of asking for help and advocating for myself, I built a wall to protect myself, to guard my heart and mind against others who might make me feel worse than I already felt.

I remember that feeling every time I meet a new student — every time I say, *"Estoy aquí para ayudarte."* And I imagine you'll use this same phrase later in life to help others facing similar needs to what you're facing right now.

It took a while, but soon you realized that I really was there to help — that my job was to help you understand what you were learning and make the class accessible for you. Soon, instead of rolling your eyes and turning away, you started turning toward me, asking for help. Then one day you hugged me as you walked into class, and I was so happy that you were beginning to trust me. The next day, you hugged me again, and we soon started getting to know each other better. You were always happy to see me, and I loved watching your walls come down.

But you were still pretty private, rarely letting me see your worries or your struggles, so when you barged into my classroom yesterday, clearly panic-stricken, I knew whatever was happening was scaring you to death.

It came out slowly. You told me you'd been seeing this boy and that you'd missed your period. You were afraid you might be pregnant.

My heart ached for you immediately. I knew how terrifying this was for you. I knew you were seeing your whole
future — all your hopes and dreams — change right
before your eyes. I also knew that I would have to share
certain parts of my own story with you. At that moment I
had two choices: put a wall up like you had done with me
before, or open my heart to you and share an experience
that would strengthen our relationship and perhaps give
you peace of mind.

I decided not to share it at that moment, mostly because
I was scared. I knew that sharing my own pregnancy
experience would help you trust me and encourage you
to let me help you, but I was worried that if I shared that
"dark side" of myself, you wouldn't look up to me as your
teacher — as a professional — anymore. So instead, I
asked you some questions about how you were feeling. I
asked this because I had some idea myself. I remembered
the confusing thoughts, the what-ifs, and the how, when,
and why. I would've loved to discuss these questions with
someone when I was going through this in my own life.
I also asked you about your relationship with this boy
and how long it had been since your missed period, and
I suggested you go to the drugstore and buy a pregnancy

test to be sure. I told you how they worked, and I told you that if it was positive, the first thing you'd need to do would be to tell your parents.

When you left my classroom, you were still panicking, but at least you had a concrete step to take — something to do to make sure. I prayed for you that night. I prayed for a negative test, of course, but mostly I prayed for you to have the courage not to put your walls back up.

When you came back into my classroom today, your panic was gone, and you were grinning from ear to ear. I knew right away you'd gotten good news from your pregnancy test. Sure enough, you pulled it out of your backpack to show me that little blue minus sign. We cheered, we celebrated, we cried, and we hugged. Then we talked about how you could avoid this kind of scare in the future.

I am so glad you came to me in this terrifying moment, Raquel. Even though the test was negative, I want to share my story with you now so you can see just how well I understood your feelings, and so you'll know that you're not alone in moments like these.

When I was twenty, I had left high school without a diploma and was working as a cashier in Queens. I had met this boy at church, and we'd started dating. He was Colombian and so good looking. I was used to short Guatemalan guys, but he was tall and cute with his Colombian afro hair. I started going out with him, and we had fun, but it wasn't anything too serious, so when I missed my period, I panicked just like you did. I was always so regular, like a ticking clock, so I knew exactly what this must mean. When I called my boyfriend, it became clear that he wasn't going to stick around. "I'm working," he said. "You figure it out."

So, I figured it out. I went to the pharmacy and bought a test. Even though I was 20 years old, I had no idea what I was doing or what to expect. I read the instructions over and over, trying to make sense of this pregnancy test while also thinking about the possibilities. Sure enough, I saw that little pink plus sign. But I *couldn't* be pregnant. It wasn't possible. I had so much to do. I was working so hard just to survive. I couldn't be pregnant, especially not with this guy who wasn't going to stay around — someone who I didn't really want to stay around anyway.

At first, I was in denial. Since I didn't know much about these at-home tests, I thought maybe I had done something wrong. So, I decided to visit the experts for a second opinion. I remember walking down some unfamiliar streets in Queens, New York, looking for the hospital. When I got there, I sat in the waiting room, alone, asking myself, "What am I going to do if it's confirmed positive?" My mind was blank. All I could think about were the "what-ifs." Fear took over, and there was no one with me to face it.

The doctor said yes, I was pregnant. Still in denial, I went to two more hospitals and got the same answer. I *still* couldn't believe it. I was not running away from the truth. It wasn't like I didn't want to accept the fact that I was having a child. I was just confused, lost, and worried about what would become of me and this baby coming into my life. Finally, I went into a clinic. In the waiting room, I watched women come and go, some excited, some panicking like me. When it was my turn, they told me the same thing I'd heard from the other three doctors: I was pregnant. They told me how far along I was, and they handed me my "option." It was a pamphlet about abortion. Without even thinking, I said, "Thank you, but no," and I walked out of the clinic. That was the moment I knew. This realization hit me so hard that my thoughts cleared up. I began thinking positively and with a different perspective. Yes, I was pregnant. Yes, I was going to have this baby. I knew I could handle it — I mean, I'd basically raised my siblings, and they'd all survived, hadn't they? It was time to face the facts and approach this like a grownup.

But first, I had to tell my mom.

I was terrified to tell her because I felt like I had failed her in so many ways. She had brought me to the United States for a better life, but I hadn't finished high school, I still didn't speak English very well, I wasn't much help with the kids anymore, and now I was pregnant. She'd made so many sacrifices for us, cleaning toilets and doing backbreaking work and everything else in her power to put food on the table and a roof over our heads, and I felt like I'd failed her. She'd given me existence and I'd become just another statistic. I was just another disappointment for her.

But, of course, my mom was wonderful. She immediately

started making plans to make sure I was healthy and find me a better place to live than my dingy apartment. When I told her my boyfriend wasn't willing to stay in the picture, she embraced me even more. She'd been there herself, with two of my siblings' fathers leaving her rather than staying to take care of the kids. She had raised her kids on her own, and she knew I could do it too.

My mom had just gotten married herself, and she couldn't take me in to live at her house. She suggested we call my Tía Rosie, who lived here in North Carolina, to see if she could help me. Tía Rosie was my grandmother's sister and more of a grandmother than my actual grandma. I was afraid of disappointing her too, but like my mama, she jumped into action. "Yes, of course," Tía Rosie said when my mom called to explain the situation. "Send her over."

So I left New York and moved in with Tía Rosie in North Carolina. I fell in love with this part of the country, and that move — not to mention the time I spent with Tía Rosie — turned out to be one of the best things that have ever happened to me, as, of course, did my son. I called my ex-boyfriend when it was almost time and told him when and where his son would be born. I didn't want to be with him myself, but if he wanted to be part of his kid's life, I wasn't going to stop him. Of course he didn't show up, but that was okay. I didn't need him, and neither did my baby. I love my son more than anything, and I would never change my past, but I'm so glad your test came back negative.

It sounds to me like you were in a similar situation — hanging out with this guy who's fun for now, but not somebody you're in love with. And at sixteen, you have so much going for you! Much more than I did when I was twenty. You have so many privileges, Raquel, as a student on your way to a high school diploma, as the only child of two doting parents who've given you everything you need. But that doesn't mean you don't struggle — I've seen it. I've seen the panic in your face when you couldn't understand what I said to you in English; I saw it in my classroom just yesterday, and I worry because I've seen you put your walls back up when things get difficult. I've also seen you ignore the challenges and rely on your privilege and your fancy clothes and your hair and makeup to get you by.

Here's what I've learned, though: pretty can buy you a drink. You can flip your hair like you always do, and you'll get what you want more often than not, at least for a while. But there's more to life than that. There will be times when you have to decide to put that pretty hair back in a ponytail, roll up your sleeves, and get to work. That's true with your education, it would have been true if your pregnancy test had been positive, and it will be true over and over again as you finish school, start your career, and build your life.

It won't be easy — nothing important is ever easy — but I know you are capable of handling hard work and making difficult decisions. I hope you know that too. More than anything, I hope that's what you'll learn from this experience.

Of course, we all need help. I was able to get help from my mom and my Tía Rosie, and I hope you'll keep letting people in when you need them. You have so much to look forward to, Raquel, and I can't wait to watch you take over the world — starting right here at school.

Your teacher always,
Ms. Francis

chapter 6

Alonso

Dear Alonso,

I'm still laughing about your phone call this morning!
How did you get on the wrong bus?! Even if it was dark
and you were tired, I can't believe remote learning lasted
so long that you forgot which school to go to! You're just
like the Guatemalan kid from that book we read — Bus
17 — ending up at the middle school instead of the
high school! We all laughed about what happened to the
character, never thinking it would actually happen to one
of us!

But all kidding aside, I was so happy to see you back in
school today. Even though you didn't need me to be in
Mrs. Gordon's class with you, I wanted to be there
to see if I could help you adjust to being back for the
second semester. When I read your free write from Mrs.
Gordon's class about what was motivating you during
this last semester of your senior year, I have to admit I

breathed a huge sigh of relief. You wrote, "The reason I am putting effort into this semester is because I want better opportunities in the future to find a better job. I want my parents to feel proud of me. I want to graduate." Reading that, I knew that all the work we did to help you stay in school while you were supporting your family last semester was worth it. I'm so happy to see how determined you still are to finish school and take advantage of all the opportunities your high school diploma will open up for you. Reading your note brought back a lot of my own high school memories as well. I remember yearning to finish school and make a better future for myself, and I also remember thinking it wasn't possible. But you've realized much more quickly than I did that, although giving up may seem like the easier road to take, the decision has much more significant impacts in the long run.

When you first joined my newcomer class last year, Alonso, you blew me away. Do you remember when we made introductions on the first day? I had you complete a name tent just like your peers had done at the beginning of the school year before you joined us. I asked you to write your name, your home country, and the languages you speak, and I told you that you could share in Spanish if you wanted, but you didn't want to. "No," you said, "I'll do it in English." And you did. Your English was still broken, but you were able to introduce yourself so beautifully that I swear my jaw was on the floor. Even though I knew that you had been born in the United States and attended a couple of years of elementary school here, you'd gone to Mexico with your parents and received most of your education there. Your English was mostly self-taught, and you were so proud of that! You were shy, but you were dedicated and determined. Your parents had sent you here to finish high school in the United States while they stayed behind in Mexico because that's what they wanted for you — and you wanted it too. You always worked so hard, and when the pandemic hit and you had to finish your junior year from home, you worked even harder. I was always so impressed, and I still have some of the work you did with me. Of course, you passed every single class. I was so proud, and I was confident that you would graduate. All you needed were a few more core courses.

So when you messaged me over the summer to tell me your parents had lost their jobs due to the pandemic and that you were planning to drop out of school and work full time to support your family back in Mexico, I was devastated. I emailed the principal and the guidance counselors right away. "We have seen this kid thrive, and we know what a good student and hard worker he is," I said. "We need to work with him to make sure he graduates this year." I thank God every day that you were willing to let me help you and that the school was able to find a way for you to keep learning remotely even when the year started in person.

You would get up early to drive 45 minutes to work at the lumber company every morning, hauling boards around outside in the sun all day, then come home late and start your schoolwork. I knew it would be a lot of work and a lot of long nights, but I also knew that you could do it, even if you weren't sure yourself. I was excited to help you achieve this dream. What I didn't tell you then was that I knew balancing school and work was possible because I did it myself when I was in high school.

You see, when I was attending high school in the United States, my mother was still in the process of obtaining legal residency, so even though she was a single mother with five children, she wasn't able to get any government support. She worked hard cleaning houses and nannying

for other families, but there was just never enough money.
The church we attended knew our circumstances and
would sometimes send us home from services with a
few bags of groceries. We also had some friends who
would drop off food occasionally, but I did most of the
grocery shopping for my family. Spaghetti was usually
affordable, so we'd eat that quite often. I also learned to
cook potato and carrot soup, which always made enough
for seconds. I would go to the C-Town Supermarket in
Floral Park, New York, and on every shopping trip, I
literally had to count my pennies to be sure I had enough
money to afford the minimum amount of food we needed
to feed all of us. There was one cashier who noticed me
counting change, and she took an interest in me. One
day, she asked me how old I was and I told her I was 15.
"You know," she said in Spanish, "you can start working
when you turn 16. When do you turn 16?" I told her my
birthday was August 31 and she said, "Come back here on
September 1st, and we'll talk to the owners about getting
you a job here." I told her I didn't speak English yet, so
I didn't think I could work in a customer service job like
that, but she just said, "Well, you have until September.
Learn as much as you can."

When people ask how I found my first job, I always tell them I didn't choose the supermarket — the supermarket chose me. As soon as I turned 16, I told that cashier I was ready to work. By then I'd learned enough English to have a social conversation, so she talked to the manager and the owners, and they gave me a job as a bagger. I started right away, standing at the end of the cash register and bagging groceries.

At first, I would just nod and smile at customers as I handed them their groceries, but I improved quickly once I got comfortable in the store. Since I've always liked to observe things, I did a lot of my learning just by watching. I think I learned to be that way because when I was younger, I spent a lot of time in the market in Guatemala with my mom, and I had to be very aware of my surroundings. I will always be grateful to my mother for teaching me this skill because it helped me become a quick learner. Even though I was not proficient in English yet, watching others always helped me learn. When I started working at the supermarket, I kept observing. I must admit that I was confused and nervous at first because our mercados in Guatemala are so different. The frozen section and the deli at the C-Town Supermarket especially intimidated me, but I quickly started learning the "supermarket language," and soon I could talk about the vegetables, the fruits, the frozen section, and the meat department all in English. I eventually started talking with the customers more. I'd say, "Good morning," or "How are you today?" when they were checking out, and after they paid, I'd ask, "Can I help you take the groceries to the car?" Soon I was so good at my job that the manager asked me to learn how to use the cash register. I learned fast, the customers loved me, and it felt so good to be doing useful work and helping my family.

I didn't work full time like you did, although I admire how incredibly selfless you were, doing everything in your power to help your parents while they were out of work. School aside, because of my little siblings, I couldn't work every day. If Mom wasn't home, then I had to be there with the kids. When she was at home, though, I would walk to the supermarket and spend my afternoons and many weekends working to bring money back to my family.

But like you, Alsonso, I had a hard time staying on top
of my schoolwork while I helped my family. When I
was in Guatemala, I could do everything because school
wasn't as challenging as it was in the United States. Here,
I was in an unfamiliar country, not only learning a new
language, but also learning about things that I had never
seen. It was a struggle for me, but it was also a struggle
for my brother and sisters, who would constantly get in
trouble for not finishing all their assignments or forgetting to bring a snack. Since they were learning English
too, I always helped them with their homework first.
When I wasn't at the supermarket, I would make them
dinner and sit with them while they studied. It wasn't
until they would sit down to watch TV or play that I
would take over the kitchen table and start doing my own
work. I usually had to drown out the noise from the TV
or my sisters' music to study, and I had to ignore my little
brother running his trucks over my books. Sometimes
teachers would scold me for turning in homework with
food on it, but I knew I was doing the best I could to
get it all done, often working past midnight just like you
did so many nights last semester. I've often wished my
mother had taken a picture of me doing my schoolwork
on one of those late nights. The little ones were asleep, so

all the lights were out except one kitchen light that let me see what I was doing. Even though there are no pictures as proof of the many hours and the late nights we worked on assignments, we know the effort we put in and how much it has mattered to us. Some nights, when it felt especially hard, I would think of my little brother and sisters and hope that they noticed my efforts and would follow in my footsteps. I know you feel the same way about your little brother.

In some ways, you had an advantage over me because you could already read and write well in English and Spanish when you started working. Nonetheless, I know it was hard for you. I can't imagine waking up at 4:00 every morning to go to work like you did. I was so impressed every night when you would text me at 9:30 to tell me you were starting your homework after a full day of work and ask me for help with things you didn't understand. When you would text again at 10:30 to tell me you were getting too sleepy to keep working, I was happy to let your teachers know you would get your assignments finished the next day because I always knew you would.

I stayed up with you all those nights because I wanted

you to have the support I didn't have when I was your age and juggling so much. There were many nights when I stayed up until three o'clock in the morning translating assignments from English to Spanish and from Spanish back to English. When I didn't know how to do something, I didn't have someone to reach out to and say, "I'm stuck on this problem. How do you do this?" I didn't have that one person whose classroom I could sneak into the next morning for help with that one last question either. If there was a teacher like that in my school, I never made a connection with her, though I do remember two ESL teachers. Every once in a while, I'd go to their classrooms, and they would be full of ESL students laughing and talking, but I never felt like I could be part of that group of students who were friends with their teachers. Looking back, sometimes I blame myself, but other times, I blame them. I know I would have felt like I could approach those teachers if they'd demonstrated some interest in me, but back then I didn't think they even knew my name. That's exactly why I made sure you always had a way to contact me. I wanted you to make sure you knew I was interested in your success and your future, and I'm glad I did. I'm also happy you reached out to me when you were thinking about dropping out.

Don't get me wrong — I'm not saying this because I want you to pity me or think, "Poor Ms. Francis!" In many ways, doing so much on my own taught me a lot of important lessons about advocating for myself, and I'm grateful for that. Even so, no matter how old we are, it's important to know there's somebody in our corner when we're going through something difficult. When it came to high school academics, I felt like I was on my own, and I never want my students to feel like that. So even when it's late at night (as long as it's before midnight!), I want you and your classmates to know that I'm here to help.

For many of us, just knowing that there's someone in the room (or on our phones) who cares about us makes a big difference in how confident and successful we can be. When I was a 15-year-old sitting at that kitchen table, I really wished I had someone like that. Now, I try to be that person for you and your fellow students. After all, you know what they say: "Be the hero you wish you had!"

Days like today make it all worth it, Alonso. Seeing your face in school now that your parents are employed again was incredible. I saw how close you came to giving up, but the fact that you didn't — that you chose to keep working toward graduation and that you're so close now — shows just how strong and capable you really are. I'm sure there will be challenges ahead in this last semester, but when things get too hard, just remember what you wrote in Mrs. Gordon's class this morning about wanting to finish school so you can graduate and have a better job. Well, you *can* have a better job — you can have *any* career you want! Keep that vision clear in your mind because the opportunities that come with a high school diploma will make all those challenges worth it. And remember that I'm here to help you if you get stuck on an assignment or need support.

Whether you want to pop into my classroom early in the morning or text me after dinner, I've got your back, and I can't wait to cheer for you as you walk across the graduation stage this spring. Just be sure you get on the right bus that morning so you don't miss the ceremony!

Your teacher <u>always</u>,

Ms. Francis

chapter 7

Marco

Dear Marco,

I'm so glad we finally got to meet in person at the soccer game! I was there with my students, cheering on their classmate Orlando. I had no idea you'd be there too. I didn't even recognize you at first! None of your photos had given me a clear picture of what you look like. I'm so happy you reached out to me online when you first started thinking about finishing your education, and it was such a joy to meet you in person. I still don't know exactly how you found me on Instagram, but I'm honored that you trusted me enough to strike up a conversation. The education system is hard to navigate without a guide and an advocate, and I'm happy to be both to the best of my abilities.

Marco, I have to admit that when I saw you at the game, my first thought was how easy it might be to judge you by your appearance — how easy it is for anybody to judge anybody by their appearance. You wore your pants hanging low, with a big, baggy shirt. You had your earrings in, and your tattoos were on full display. Your hat was sideways, and you walked with this swagger, giving off a vibe that you were too cool for everyone around you. It would be so easy for so many people to write you off, to say, "No wonder he dropped out of school." And maybe that's what you want. Maybe you present yourself a certain way as a defense mechanism — a way to beat them to the punch.

But guess what? When I saw you in the park yesterday, that wasn't my first impression. I had already gotten to know you from our Instagram conversations, and I could see beyond your tattoos and your outfit and your facial expressions. I knew your heart. I knew your background. I knew you dared to face the workforce here in the United States as an adult would even though you're a teenage boy. You'd come to the United States with the idea of starting school and being successful, but you were burdened with the responsibility of having to work to make money at the same time. When school got hard for you, you had the courage to choose to do what you needed to do to provide for yourself and your grandmother back in Mexico.

When I first learned your story, I had two options. I could
have felt bad for you. I could've pitied you for being so
young and feeling like you couldn't continue your education. Or, I could have done what I decided to do instead:
praise you for the difficult decisions you've made. Because
I had seen your strength, I was so excited to meet you and
talk to you in person, to tell you how amazed I am by the
way you've created the life you think is best for yourself.

I am so inspired by your initiative, but I also know you
may not want to work in construction for the rest of your
life. Or maybe you will want to stay in construction, but
you'll want to move over to the business side or even
manage your own team. Either way, there's a good chance
that what you're doing right now won't work for you
in five years, so I want you to have a backup plan that
ensures whatever path you want to take is still open to
you.

I know I've told you on Instagram how important I think
it is for you to continue your education. I want you to
continue learning English and taking ESL classes so
you'll have the ability to communicate here in the United

States, even if it's just to order coffee at Dunkin' Donuts or Starbucks. But I hope you'll also keep working toward your GED, because the process of earning one will give you a little more knowledge and a little more learning. Once you have it, that certificate will open up a new world of opportunities — for college courses, graduate programs, and access to many other jobs.

You know I dropped out of high school just like you did. You also know I eventually went back to school and earned my master's degree. But you don't know the whole story. You don't know how close I came to giving up or how getting my GED truly turned my life around. I could tell when we talked yesterday that you were feeling a little discouraged, so I want to show you what's still possible for you by sharing my story now.

In my senior year of high school, I had to take Regents Exams in all of my classes. These are just like the end-of-course exams we take here in North Carolina, except that in New York, failing a Regents Exam meant you couldn't graduate. I passed every single exam: reading, writing, science, biology…every exam except American History. Every time I got a passing score, I felt so great. It was a real accomplishment, and it was another reassurance that I could do this. But the failing grade on that American History test meant none of the other tests mattered. I took it three times — twice in English and once in Spanish. After that last time, my counselor called me into the office and said I'd used up all my chances. I couldn't retake the test until it was offered again the next spring. In the meantime, I already had all the course credits I needed to graduate, and because I was already eighteen, I couldn't register for any more classes. According to the counselor, if I wanted my diploma, my only option was just to go home and spend the next year studying to retake the exam. If I passed then, I would finally be able to graduate.

I was so disappointed. I had given everything I had and worked as hard as I could. I had learned a whole new language, and I had done so well on all my other exams, but because of this one test, I had nothing to show for it.

When I left school that afternoon, I walked straight to a friend's house. He'd just come to the United States from Nicaragua that year, and he'd managed to pass the test. I asked him how he did it, and he pulled out this enormous textbook. It was so big he even struggled to carry it. "You read that whole thing?" I asked. He said he had. He offered to loan me the book, but I knew there was no way I could read it all. (Of course, he'd learned English before he came to the United States, so even though I'd been here longer, he had a leg up in his reading ability.) Even if the language wouldn't be a challenge, I didn't have time to spend a whole year reading. I had to earn money to help support my family, and I had to help my mom take care of my siblings.

So, I gave up on school.

I'd worked part time all through high school, but at this point I entered the workforce full time. I worked as a cashier at C-town Supermarket and was very good at my job. I had a lot of energy and was great at customer service. Soon, I got promoted to taking phone orders, and it felt good to use the English I had learned. I was making good money, and I liked that feeling. I could buy my own car and pay for my own car insurance, and I could even afford the rent to live in my own place. I had put school behind me. I wasn't going back. I had accepted that the door had closed on the opportunities I had always dreamed of, thanks to that one American History test.

I don't know what your dream is, Marco, but let me tell you about mine. One time, when I was working at the market in Guatemala — I must have been nine or ten years old — a teacher walked by me with her students. She was nicely dressed, and the way she walked, she looked like a model on the catwalk. She was so sophisticated, so put together, so professional, and her students were just following along in this neat little line, like ducklings behind their mama. I didn't know anything about her, but I could tell by watching her that her life was very different from mine. I knew that what she did wasn't a job like selling at the market — it was a profession. I knew at that moment that I wanted to be just like her, even though I didn't know what it was like to have a classroom or to teach. Seeing that teacher walking by with her students, so confident and poised, sparked that dream, and I knew that one day, I was going to find out.

When I left high school, I forgot about that dream for a while. It no longer seemed like it was within reach. In reality, although I'd buried that dream as deep as I could, it kept nudging me. Sometimes my unrealized dream

made me regret all the effort I'd put into my years in
school, and sometimes it made me daydream of a life I
believed had become impossible due to my circumstances.

A couple of years later, when I was twenty years old, I got
pregnant and moved to North Carolina to live with my
Tía Rosie. When I got here, I started looking for jobs. I
was looking for what we called *trabajos limpios*. "Clean
jobs"
were jobs like receptionist or cashier that you wouldn't
have to be ashamed of, as opposed to jobs like attending
bathrooms, but almost everything I applied for required a
high school diploma.

Even when they didn't require a diploma, there was
always something else that held me back. I remember
applying for jobs at banks and thinking how cool it would
be to work in a nice clean place like that. Some banks I
applied for required a test of how fast you could count
money and process information. I'm not sure if it was my
lack of confidence or lack of English proficiency, but I
was never able to pass those tests either.

Another job I applied for was at an insurance office. All I was supposed to do was answer calls and sell the product. When I started practicing for the position, I was intimidated by the people on the other side of the line. I remember thinking, "What if they ask me something I can't understand?" and "What if I can't remember everything I'm supposed to know?" So I called the next day and told the office manager I wasn't interested.

After that phone call, I realized I was not ready for the workforce even though I had completed my years in high school. I was not ready to contribute to society. I was scared and confused, and I felt useless.

But you know, Marco, we shouldn't need a diploma to feel useful. We shouldn't need a diploma to feel prepared to serve our society. What we need is the feeling that we matter, a sense of belonging in this country, and a clear idea that who and what we are can impact those around us.

It was Tía Rosie who finally mentioned the GED. "Okay," she said, "before you have this kid, why don't you see if you can get your GED?" I had no idea what she was talking about, so she explained it to me. In three to six months, I could get the equivalent of a high school diploma — what I'd worked so hard for in the past three years and had come to believe was no longer an option. At first I was furious that nobody had told me about this before. Why hadn't the high school counselor told me I had another choice? To this day, I wish someone would've taken five minutes of their day to call me and lay out my options. A principal or a guidance counselor or my ESL teacher could've called. The social worker could have called. But it's like they didn't even notice I was gone. Didn't they even care that I wasn't coming back or graduating? Didn't they care about my future?

Until Tía Rosie suggested the GED, I had believed I'd become a simple statistic who would just have to face life. Now, though, I was excited to finally move forward with my life and I got to work right away. I wanted to continue my education, both for the baby and for myself. I needed to prove I was capable, that I wasn't the failure I had believed myself to be when I became a high school dropout.

I now realize that taking this initiative allowed me to write a different and more positive personal narrative. This was the point when I picked up the pen. Before, I had let people dictate my journey, but now, it was all up to me whether I made it or not.

Once I'd earned my GED, I was able to get back on track to achieve my dream of becoming a teacher. But believe it or not, obtaining my GED didn't give me the confidence I needed to apply for college right away. The feelings of failure in my heart and mind were still strong and doubt took over me again. While I was satisfied knowing that there was a certificate in my drawer that could one day allow me to apply for college, I still felt incapable. All I could think about was how I had worked so hard to demonstrate my potential in high school and it still wasn't enough. I let failure destroy even the way I saw myself. I was still letting a diploma — or lack thereof — dictate my limits.

I applied for my associate's degree, and at the same time, I applied to work within Cabarrus County Schools. That seed that had been planted in my heart when I was little was starting to sprout again. I'm sure you've heard the famous quote, "*Quisieron enterrarnos, pero no sabían que éramos semillas.*"

"They tried to bury us, but they didn't know we were seeds."

When I see that quote, I think "they" refers to the entire system of adults and staff members who surrounded me back then but never really cared. I also think of my own inner fears and negative thoughts and my way of thinking and looking at life.

Maybe you've had similar thoughts, Marco, but just like me, you came to the United States with a mission! We came here not to burden others, not to expect others to do things for us or hand us things. We came here because we knew we were capable of achieving anything we wanted to work for. The seed in that quote is our resilience, and if we let it, it eventually sprouts and grows to impact those around us.

Thanks to that sprouting seed, I was desperate to get my foot in the door of the education system. Don't ask me how, but I knew I could be a great educator. At least, I knew that I could be helpful in a school setting. I didn't care much about the details; I just wanted to make a difference, so I applied to work either as a custodian or on the cafeteria staff. I knew how to clean and cook, so I didn't see why I shouldn't get one of those positions, but on the spur of the moment, I also applied to be a teacher's assistant. I knew I wasn't qualified, but I thought it wouldn't hurt to try.

To my surprise, I got an interview for the teacher's assistant job. Because I had never interviewed for such a fancy position, I didn't own any appropriate clothing. The first thing I did was go to the mall and buy the nicest shirt and pants I could find. I still remember the outfit so vividly. I also did a little research on how to respond to interview questions. I had never been interviewed formally, so I wanted to be prepared.

When they asked about my experience, I said, "I don't know how to read a lot of English. I can't even write a whole lot of English. I couldn't teach right now if you asked me to. But let me tell you what I do know: I know how to take care of kids. I raised my siblings on my own for several years, and they survived. I fed them. I cleaned them. I bathed them. And they're alive, each one of them. So, if you leave me in a classroom with kids, they will survive. That's all I can tell you." I made the interviewers laugh, but I knew there was no way they would hire me.

But they did.

I worked as a teaching assistant and a bus driver while I was earning my associate's degree. Those were long days for me. I would crank up my bus at 5:30 a.m., work as a teaching assistant from 8:00 to 3:00, and drive students back home until 4:30. I would then go to Rowan Cabarrus Community College to work on my degree, which was required to keep my teaching assistant position. I would get home around 9:30 in the evening. Then, my weekends were for school work. My son was three years old at the time, and I was lucky to have a very supportive family who helped me with him while I attended school.

I learned everything I could about teaching during that time, and I worked hard to improve my academic English. Sitting in a first-grade classroom, I would take notes as the teacher taught her first graders. I learned rules of the English language that I didn't know. I learned chants and heard books read aloud that I'd never heard of before. I was exposed to celebrations and content knowledge I didn't even know I was missing. I began to embrace learning and studying in a first-grade classroom. Among other things, I was becoming an educator.

I completed my associate's degree at Rowan-Cabarrus Community College in 2007. Walking across that stage to receive my diploma — the first I'd earned in the United States — was such a powerful experience. It reaffirmed that I could be successful and achieve my dreams. The sense of failure I'd been carrying since that day in the high school counselor's office finally began to lift. Courage and self-advocacy started to gain strength in me.

I remember dropping off my enrollment form at the University of North Carolina, where I wanted to continue my education. The receptionist asked me for my high school transcripts. Of course, I didn't have them because I was not enrolling with my high school records but with my GED. When I told the receptionist this, she told me that I couldn't enroll at a university with just a GED and that I was wasting my time. Rather than be discouraged when she tried to dismiss me, I summoned my courage and confidence and said, "I have an associate's degree from RCCC, and this allows me to enroll at the university and pursue the career of my choice." She apologized, looked at my records again, and processed my enrollment.

You see, this is exactly what education gives us: the power to protect and advocate for ourselves — the ability to speak up and show our true potential.

So I enrolled at the University of North Carolina to earn my bachelor's degree in elementary education, but my challenges weren't over. I had to pass a test called the PRAXIS to be admitted to the college of education. Just like with the American History test, I hit a wall. I took it six times, and I failed every time. My academic English was so much better, but it still wasn't good enough. Eventually, it took another teacher to highlight my specific weakness. While I was preparing myself to retake the PRAXIS test, I took the electives required for a bachelor's degree. In an art class I was taking, I was required to turn in a written assignment. I felt pretty proud of my work, but when I received my paper back, it was full of red ink. At the top, the professor had written, "You'll never graduate from this university writing like this!" It hurt. It was disappointing. At some points in the process, I felt so beaten down that I was ready to give up. Sometimes that seemed easier than continuing to struggle uphill, but I was tired of failures. I was tired of doors being slammed right in front of me. Besides, by this time, I'd learned something important that I hadn't known when I was in high school: there are always other options, and you can find them if you know how to speak up for yourself.

I didn't have the confidence or power as a high school senior to tell the guidance counselor that what she was asking me to do was impossible. I didn't have the guts to tell her I had other responsibilities that meant I couldn't just go home, get a book, and spend all my time studying. But by the time I'd reached the university level, I had gained confidence, self-respect, and the self-advocacy tools to fight for what I believed in and for what I knew I was capable of.

So, after all my advisors repeatedly told me the only way to enroll in the department of education was to pass the PRAXIS, I gave up on them, not on myself!

Their inability to help me and the limitations they were setting for me wouldn't affect me like they did back in high school. I went to the guidance office and asked the secretary, "Would you make me an appointment with the person in charge of all of the guidance counselors? I don't want any of the counselors because I've seen all of them. I want the person in charge." She must've realized I wasn't going anywhere until I got what I wanted because she made me an appointment, no questions asked. When I walked in, the head of the counseling department was very welcoming, but when I explained my situation and how I couldn't pass the PRAXIS test, he started with the same old story: "Well, you really need to take this test. If you don't pass this test, I am afraid you can't register for any of these classes."

But this time, I put my foot down. I said, "No, I'm not leaving your office. You have to have an option. I walked out of Martin Van Buren High School at eighteen thinking there were no options, only to find out years later that there was an option, and they just didn't bother telling me." I said, "Look in your drawers, look in your computer. I know there is a way." I heard my voice come out strong, and I felt so confident. I was proud of myself. I knew

I wasn't being rude; I was just stating my needs and demanding opportunities. This is exactly what we need as immigrants in the United States: opportunities to show our abilities and to give back to our society. I remember keeping my eyes on him the entire time. I didn't want pity — I wanted solutions. I wanted to learn what possibilities were available to me.

That's when he finally understood that I wasn't about to give up on my dream of becoming a teacher, and he started problem-solving with me. Even better, he introduced me to a specific kind of teaching I had never considered as a possibility for me. He understood that I was struggling to pass this test because English isn't my first language, and he told me there was a profession for teaching kids just like me — kids who didn't speak English and needed to learn in order to succeed in school. He started pulling out all the information about this program for teaching English as a second language. Of course I'd had ESL teachers in high school, so I knew this profession existed, but becoming an ESL teacher had never crossed my mind. All of a sudden, I began seeing the light at the end of my dark tunnel...until I realized what he was showing me was all part of the department of education. My heart sank once again. Fortunately though, this man had found my option. "What I'm showing you here," he said, "is a graduate degree. A master's in teaching English as a second language." He explained that all I had to do was get my bachelor's degree — majoring in anything — then come back and enroll as a graduate student in the department of education. Then, I could take any of these courses and earn my teaching degree. Since I would be working and only attending school part-time, it would mean three to four more years of school than I'd planned, but halfway through earning my master's, I would earn my license and could finally start teaching.

There it was. The opportunity, the possibility, the path I could take to obtain my teaching license. My mind started racing, filled with images of having my own class-room and helping students who were struggling with the same battles I had faced as an English learner. I shook the department head's hand and thanked him profusely. I had known there must be an option, and he had helped me find it.

Fast forward a few years: I'd gotten my license and been

offered a job in Cabarrus County, and the assistant principal of my new school was giving me a tour. We walked
into a room, and he said, "This is your classroom." I had
dreamed about and planned for this moment for years,
and those words were music to my ears. I asked for a
moment alone and I stood in my classroom, imagining
it all decorated and full of students, imagining the way
kids would walk in and say, "Hello, Mrs. Francis." At that
moment, I felt just like that teacher walking through the
market in Guatemala. I had finally made it.

All of this taught me two things that I think would be
helpful for you, Marco. First, it's never too late to change
your life. The GED opened the doors that empowered
me to transform my journey, and I know it will do the
same for you. Second, you have to be able to stand up for
yourself. I know you know how to do that because you've
already accomplished so much. But you'll have to keep
it up because it's likely going to be even harder for you,
as an undocumented student, to open up those doors for
yourself. I am going to help you out as much as possible.
Right now I'm in the process of trying to find out how
to get you enrolled in community college, even without
documentation. I'll try to help you and other students like

you however I can, but when it's all said and done, you're the only one who can make things happen for yourself.

Too often, I think people judge us based on what they think we cannot do, and too often, we buy into those negative perceptions and limit ourselves. But when I look at you, I don't see deficits. I see strengths. And I hope you do too. I see your sweetness. I see a person who cares, who wants something better than what he has. I see someone who works hard to make money to send back to his grandma in Mexico because he knows how difficult life is back home.

I can't say I understand your specific situation because I don't. I've been documented the entire time I've lived in this country, and I know that has removed certain obstacles for me that you still have to face. But I've seen undocumented immigrants find jobs, survive, and help others survive with the money they make. It is possible. The more you can educate yourself, the more doors will open for you. The more you learn — English and anything else — the more prepared you'll be to succeed under any circumstances you encounter, whether you stay here in the United States or go back to Mexico one day.

It may seem useless, breaking your back for your GED when you aren't even sure you can stay in the United States. However, here's how I see it: if you have to go back to Mexico, you can go back and be uneducated and unable to read and write, or you can go back and say, "I have a United States high school diploma, and I can read and write in English." In Mexico, just like here, that piece of paper will afford you so many more opportunities to build the life you want.

I know you're discouraged right now, but I know you can do it. Look at you — you're building houses! If you can do that, you can definitely do the work to get your GED.

And remember, whenever you need help finding your options, you need encouragement, or you just need to vent, I'll be right there on Instagram, just a few clicks away.

Your teacher *always* (even if not officially),

Ms. Francis

chapter 8

Jaime

Dear Jaime,

When you told me this morning that you were going to miss class tomorrow because you were going to get your picture taken for your United States passport, I don't know which one of us was more excited. (Well, you, of course, but I was a close second!) We celebrated and cheered in my classroom, and now, hours later, I'm still celebrating for you. I know how scared you've been over the last few months, wondering if you would get sent back to Guatemala but, but now that you know you're safe, and I couldn't be happier or more proud of you.

It's been so much fun to watch you grow since that first day of the summer class I taught for high school newcomers. I was an elementary teacher at the time, but they'd asked me to step in, and I figured that if I could teach English to fifth graders, I could teach English to high school students. But that first morning, when your classmates started coming into the room, I realized I was just as nervous as most of them looked. Everyone was quiet and timid, staring at their desks or phones, fidgeting as they waited for class to start. I couldn't help but think that everyone looked and felt exactly how I had felt when I started school in the United States at 15 years old. I saw the same fear and intimidation I had felt, and I saw the same worry that the teacher would talk to me in a language I didn't understand yet. I saw the overwhelming culture shock that comes from navigating not only a new language but a new country as well.

The anxiety was contagious, and I started thinking, "Who am I to make them feel comfortable when I don't feel comfortable myself?" Then you walked in with so much energy, and you started talking to me in Spanish right away. "*¡Hola! ¿Cómo está? ¡Buenos días!*" It was a lot of energy for eight o'clock in the morning, but you put a smile on my face and made me feel so much more relaxed. I thought, "I got this."

One of our first activities was a game where we all created our own visual bios, complete with the flags from our home countries and details about ourselves, to help us all get to know one another. When you got up to

share your bio — in English, I might add, after you'd
only been in the United States three months — I was
amazed. Yours looked exactly like mine. You had included
the Guatemalan flag and our national bird, *el quetzal*,
and that was just the start. The more I learned about
you throughout the class, the more similar I realized
we were. Just like me, you came from Guatemala as an
unaccompanied, undocumented minor. You were caught
by immigration just like I was, and you were claimed by
a documented relative just like I was. Your stories about
traveling to Mexico in the back of a truck — scared and
uncomfortable — were so similar to mine. And it wasn't
just our parallel experiences either. You were so much like
me in so many ways: your excitement to be here in the
United States, the way you appreciated education and
new opportunities and a new life, and the way you were
so eager to take advantage of everything in front of you.

Getting to know you, hearing your stories, and seeing
so much of myself in you was so powerful. I don't think
you know how much you impacted my life that summer,
Jaime, but it's because of you that I moved from teaching
elementary school to teaching high school. I knew that I
wanted to help you and students like you — those who

had limited English and would soon age out of high
school — by making sure they could succeed in their
classes and acquire the credits they needed to graduate.
I felt compelled to support you and your newcomer
classmates so you all could have the same opportunities I
had (with much less drama, I hope) to achieve whatever
it is you want to achieve. You didn't even know you were
doing it, but you encouraged me to make one of the most
significant decisions of my life: to become a high school
ESL teacher.

You shared so much of your story with me, and it changed
me. To thank you, I want to tell you my story now.

Like you, I left Guatemala as a teenager. I was fifteen
years old, and I was traveling with two of my four
younger siblings. My mom was already in the United
States, and my youngest siblings' dad had sent the two
littlest ones over already. Still, we'd never really imagined
my mother being able to bring all five of us to the United
States to be with her. We knew we would eventually
be reunited, but we thought it would be back home in
Guatemala.

When my mother mentioned the possibility of us traveling to the United States, the idea was more than my mind could handle, especially the thought of traveling with a total stranger who would be receiving all mom's savings in return for a promise to bring us to her safe and sound. The adults were doing all the planning, and I felt like I hadn't had enough time to process the idea. All we were told was to pack up our essentials. I had heard terrible stories of undocumented, unaccompanied minors setting out for the United States and never making it to their destinations. As the day we were supposed to leave approached, I felt a lot of fear and doubt, but I knew my mother had made the decision for us, and I trusted her to do everything possible to give us our best chance. So I put aside the fear and made sure my sisters and I were prepared to go whether we were ready or not!

On the morning my two sisters and I left our little shack in mid-November of 1993, a lady picked us up in her car. We didn't know exactly who she was or where we were headed, but we knew this was the first part of our trip to the United States. As the car pulled up, I vividly remember holding my sisters' hands. Each of us carried

a backpack with our essentials, and we were armed with
the hope that getting into that vehicle would be the
beginning of a journey that would end with us embracing
our mother in Queens, New York. The lady took us to
her house, where we waited for the *coyote* to pick us up.
Our smuggler was big and serious, and he looked like he
meant business. When he came to pick us up, he brought
his wife, who was expecting a baby. She was very friendly
and helped us get our belongings in the car even though
it seemed like her baby was due any minute!

They brought us to their house, which had several rooms
occupied by people who were clearly not part of the
family (we could tell right away because they had back-
packs like ours.) Our room had a couple of small cots
and a coffee table. There was nothing fancy on the walls
except a picture frame with a Bible verse. I already knew
the verse very well, but during my time living in that
room, it became core to my prayers and my hope during
our journey.

We ate all of our meals in the coyote's house. We were
there for several days, watching different people come
and go. Like us, all of these people had paid the coyote to

bring them to the United States, and like us, they were holding on to hope that he would keep his promise.

About three weeks later, we were introduced to a different coyote. This one would be traveling with us from Mexico to the United States. The first couple drove us to his place to meet him so we would know him before we met again in Mexico.

He was tall, skinny, and very quiet. He kept mostly to himself, but he was a kind man who was trying to earn to a living just like anybody else. He had a family in Guatemala, and we met his wife and children before we left.

Once our passports were ready, we started the journey to Mexico City. We traveled in cars, buses, and trains for hours, and we walked quite a bit too. We stayed in Mexico City for several weeks while our coyote waited for the green light to take us to the airport. We stayed in hotels, motels, and houses, packing our bags anytime our coyote told us it was time to go to another location.

During the days, we explored Mexico City. We went around to *mercados* and tried Mexican food. We were amazed how spicy it was compared to Guatemalan food! We bought little souvenirs that we could bring to our mom and our other siblings, and we looked around for things that were similar to what we knew back home. Most days, we probably just looked like three sisters on vacation.

But every single night in bed, I got scared, afraid my sisters and I wouldn't wake up the next day. We were in an unfamiliar place with unfamiliar people, and we'd heard so many stories about kidnapping and rape — so many stories of people who tried to make it to the United States only to find themselves worse off than before. Every night I stayed awake until my sisters were asleep, then I drifted off too, hoping and praying that tomorrow would be the day we would go to the United States.

I don't know what got you through your journey, Jaime, but two things sustained me on mine. The first was my excitement to see my mom and reunite our family after so many years. The second was the picture that hung in our room in the first coyote's house, where we stayed before leaving Guatemala. The picture was a beautiful landscape with trees and a waterfall. It looked so peaceful. And the picture frame was engraved with a verse from the Bible: "*Yo soy el camino, la verdad, y la vida.*" I took a mental photo of that picture and that frame, and I told my sisters to do the same. Every night we were away from home and separated from our mom, we remembered that verse, and we believed that God would make a way for us to get to the United States.

Finally, on January 22, 1994, our coyote told us he had all of our documents ready. He showed us the passports, the plane tickets — everything. We studied the passports carefully, practicing all the information on them so we could recite everything confidently as we went through customs.

We went to bed that night in a dingy, uncomfortable motel room, knowing that the next day, we would be flying to New York City. We would finally get to see our mom.

The following morning, we packed our bags, tucking away all our little souvenirs and matching Mexican jackets, and dressed in our nicest outfits. When we got to the airport, we got on the plane without any difficulty. My sisters and I sat together, and our coyote sat a few rows away. We felt so independent and grown-up, but more than anything else, we were relieved that our journey was almost over.

Five hours after takeoff, we landed at JFK Airport in New York. We got off the plane and got in the customs line, passports in hand. I felt my body shaking, and my thoughts were all unclear. I was scared. I knew we were doing something wrong, and I felt like I was forgetting the details I was supposed to remember. As we stood there waiting our turn with the customs agent, I began to wonder: what if we get caught? What if we have to go back to Guatemala? What would we do now that my mother had spent all her savings bringing us here? I could hear my heartbeat picking up speed, and I felt short of breath. It was a feeling I never wanted to experience again.

The customs agent asked us all the questions we knew he would ask: "*¿Cómo te llamas? ¿Cuántos años tienes? ¿Qué vas a hacer en Nueva York?*" We answered just like we had practiced, but I guess we must have said something wrong, or he noticed something about with our passports or something reflected in our faces that indicated we weren't telling the truth. Instead of letting us through, he took my sisters and me to a little room while some other people took our coyote to a different room. We waited and waited, but nothing was happening, and then all of a sudden, we could see through the window that our coyote was being taken away in handcuffs, head down, by two officials.

That's when my sisters and I started crying. We knew we were busted. Somehow, they'd figured out the truth, and we were sure they were going to send us back to Guatemala. Then, the agents came in and started asking us questions. "Where is your mom? What is her address?" We really didn't know the address, and besides, our coyotes had told us not to give away any addresses or phone numbers if we got caught. Since my mom was undocumented, they would likely go after her if we did. So we just cried and begged. "Please don't send us back," I said. "We came here to be with our mother. She's all we have. There's nobody else back home." But they didn't care. They just told us that we would have to go back since we didn't have the proper documentation. "Go back to what?" I thought. Back to the shack? Back to waiting for mom to return to Guatemala, or for her to save more money so we could do it all over again? How easy they made it sound.

How easy it was for these agents to just say, "You don't belong here. Go back to where you belong." Who were they to determine our destiny? Who were they to assume that we were better off going back home than entering the United States undocumented?

They took our fingerprints, but then they kept us in that little room while officials went in and out, talking to each other but not telling us anything. Hours passed, we didn't know how many, and we were terrified. We'd seen our coyote get taken away in handcuffs, and we were afraid the same would happen to us.

This was definitely a moment when I could've helped my little sisters by staying strong, but it was too hard. All I wanted to do was cry. All I wanted, just like my little sisters, was our mother. We were tired. We were exhausted from playing adults. At that moment, we allowed ourselves to be the kids we really were, and and we all just hugged each other and started crying.

But then, two ladies came in and started talking to the officials. We didn't know who they were at first, but they were looking and pointing at us. We soon learned they were my grandmother (my mom's mom) and her sister, my Tía Rosie. I had never met my Tía Rosie in person, but I had heard of her, and we had met her dad back in Guatemala. I had seen my grandmother a couple of times, but I didn't recognize her at that moment. My grandfather, my mother's father, had taken my mom away from grandma when my mom was a little girl, leaving my grandmother heartbroken. After several years of searching for my mother and not finding her, my grandmother moved to the United States. Later, her family finally found my mother, but it was too late for them to have a real mother-daughter relationship at that point. Though she had always kept tabs on my mom, she hardly ever reached out. She couldn't bear the pain. But now, here she was at the airport, rescuing my sisters and me.

Back then, it seemed like a miracle that she and Tía Rosie knew where to find us. I learned much later that my mom's pastor was supposed to pick us up from the airport that day, but when several hours passed and we didn't come out, he called my mom to let her know something must be wrong. Mom couldn't come to get us herself because she was undocumented, so she called Tía Rosie. Then Tía Rosie and the pastor called my grandmother,

and before you know it, they were on their way to
the airport.

As you know from your own time in *la hielera*, some
undocumented immigrants can be released legally into
the United States if they have relatives to "claim" them.
These relatives prove they can provide shelter and finan-
cial support so the immigrants won't become a burden
on the government. My grandmother wasn't a citizen,
but she was a legal resident, she owned her house, and
she had a hefty savings account and a respected career
as an educator. So even though she never did support us
once we entered the United States, what mattered at that
moment was that she could.

The officials eventually let her take us with her, and so,
twelve hours after our plane landed, we walked out of
the airport and into New York. We finally got home to
my mom, and I'll never forget that first hug. We were
over the moon. We spent all that night together, talking,
laughing, and recounting our stories, so grateful to be
together — for good this time.

Jaime, you've already overcome many of the challenges I still had ahead of me when I finally made it to my grandma's house that night. But we're lucky, you and I. You see, in coming here without documentation, we were both doing something the law said was wrong. Even though we were doing what we believed we had to do, we ended up being arrested and detained. We could have been sent right back to Guatemala, but thanks to our families, we were both able to get legal documentation, and we were both able to stay. Now we can live in this country without the fear of *la migra*.

I know not all the students in your class can live without that fear, but I want you and all of your classmates to know that, no matter what you're going through, no matter what documents you have or don't have, I'm here for you. For all of you.

Smile for that passport photo, Jaime. You deserve it.

Your teacher <u>always</u>,

Ms. Francis

chapter 9

Epilogue

Dear Students,

Now that you've read my story and the stories of your fellow students, I want to tell you one more: I want to tell you about why I share my story and why I hope you will too. Remember the interview I had for the teacher's assistant position? I didn't know the first thing about teaching, so I just told the interviewers about my experiences keeping my siblings alive, healthy, and relatively happy. I haven't told you yet, but that the interview was the first time I ever told my story to someone else.

I didn't know anything about the job I was interviewing for — much less how to get it! I was so nervous about the questions they might ask that I decided to look up possible questions just so I could be prepared. When I Googled "How to interview for a teacher's assistant position," the advice that came up in search results most often was, "Just sell yourself. Talk about yourself." That made me feel so much better because, even though I didn't know much about teaching, I was an expert on myself. I could talk about my experiences, what I'd lived through, and where I was right at that moment. So I did. I didn't tell the interviewers everything I've said in these letters. I boiled it down to the basics: that I stayed back in Guatemala with my four siblings, taking care of them while Mom was gone, that I came here to the United States and put myself through most of high school while taking care of the kids at home, that I dropped out of high school because I couldn't pass that one exam, and yet here I am now. I must admit that it wasn't easy, not only because my English was not very proficient, but also because reliving my life experiences was hard. It took so much courage to expose parts of myself that I've never shared before, but it was at that moment I realized that my journey was what made me who I was and would guide me toward who I was meant to be.

I didn't know how they would react — if they would judge me or laugh at me or pity me, or if it would be enough. On the way home from the interview, my husband asked me how I felt about it. I was honest when I said, "I don't think I got the job." I knew I didn't have the experience they were looking for, but the fact that I had been allowed to share my story made me so happy. That was the very first time since I'd come to the United States that someone — anyone — had said, "Tell me your story," or "Tell me about your experiences," or even just, "Tell me about you!"

I couldn't stop thinking about the power of these questions. For the interviewers, they were just requirements to fulfill a position, but to me, they were the spark I needed to light a fire in my heart and mind. From that day on, I began embracing every single experience I'd faced. In fact, I went home that evening and started digging through all my photographs and reliving those special moments in my life.

Of course, it turned out that I had shared what those interviewers wanted to hear: that I was responsible and trustworthy enough to work with children and support a teacher. Telling my story that day also turned out to be the hook I needed to get that job.

The second time I told my story, I had been teaching for four years and was named Teacher of the Year for my school, W.M. Irvin Elementary school, here in North

Carolina. As teacher of the year at my school, I competed against all Cabarrus County schools' teachers of the year for the honor of district teacher of the year. As part of that process, I told my story again. Of course, I had a little more to say at that time because by then I had put myself through community college, I had my master's degree, and I had taught school for three years.

Not holding back felt good. Bragging about my accomplishments felt good. Highlighting all the wonderful things I was doing for my school and my community felt rewarding.

My story that brought me to another milestone two weeks later, when I was named the 2016 Cabarrus County District teacher of the year.

The local newspaper came over to interview me about the award, and they wanted to know more about me. Once again, I told my story.

At this point, my story has become core to what, how, and why I do what I do. Even though I've shared it hundreds of times now — to students, to newspapers and magazines, at teaching conferences, on my blog, and even on national television — it's never become easy. I've taken my mom with me to several of my keynote presentations across the country, and every time I get off the stage, she scolds me for crying while I tell the story. "But Mama," I say, "you try to tell our story without crying!" I even cried writing these letters, telling this story to you. It's just that emotional for me, and the more I tell it, the more it stays fresh and alive.

So if it's that emotional, why do I tell it so often? Well, there are two big reasons.

First, it helps me continue to appreciate what I've been through instead of taking my difficult experiences for granted. I think we protect those painful pieces too much because we think that talking about them will hurt us more, or will hurt the person listening. But I have learned to embrace the pain of those experiences, and I have learned to see suffering as a series of stepping stones to something higher rather than something that makes me someone to be pitied. So, when I tell my story, even though it's hard, I don't do it so people will feel sorry for me. Instead, I want the message — to myself and my audience — to be, "Hey! I was able to make it through that."

Even though hundreds might have had similar experiences and challenges, we each make those challenges unique in how we internalize them and share them (or choose not to). I know some people who decide to keep their stories to themselves because it is easier not to explain or relive their experiences, but storytelling has influenced me so much. In a way, it has allowed me to take back what was mine. Embracing my own story and seeing the value in my experiences has helped me learn to appreciate my life and the person I have become.

It seems like if you don't remember where you come from — if you don't keep that memory alive — it dies. You start devaluing your experiences. I've seen other people in my life forget where they came from, and I never want to do that. I think that remembering our suffering and what we've been through has helped my family and me stay compassionate and helped us hold onto that fire that brought us to the United States in the first place. It wasn't just to make money. It was to live a better and healthier life. If we can keep that fire in our hearts, we can pass it on to others because we never know when we might encounter someone who is going through the same things we've been through. If we want to use our experiences to help others, they've got to be alive within us.

That brings me to the second reason I share my story: to inspire others. I have shared my story with many different audiences, and I see it as a service. Every time I share it, I try to highlight the pieces that will connect with each audience. For example, when I spoke at a community college, I used the experience of getting my GED and going through a community college on my way to a university to inspire the students. If I can find a way to use my story to inspire a teacher, a kid, or anyone else, then that makes it worth telling.

I first realized how powerful telling my story could be when I shared a written version with a teacher friend to show her newcomer class. It was the first time I'd told every detail, just like I've shared with you here, and I was nervous about it until my friend shared one student's response video with me. This one student, Wanda, was going through exactly what I had experienced, and as I watched her video response, it was like I was hearing

about myself. She shared several things she found inter-
esting in my story and all the ways she connected with it,
even saying she thought my story was admirable. Wow! I
had always thought that word was just for amazing folks
who made a world of difference, but here was this young
woman using it to describe me. She saw my perseverance
and persistence as admirable. Wanda said that after
hearing my story, she felt like she could get close to me,
and she especially identified with my struggle to pass my
American History test. She had just taken the same test,
and she was worried about it. But what really hit me was
when she said, "When you listen to someone like this, it
inspires you to do more. If I put my effort into it, I can do
it too."

I identified with this student, and I saw myself in her.
More importantly, she saw herself in me, and she saw
who I had become even after all I went through. Often,
we newcomers tend to feel isolated because we are
overwhelmed by all the new things we have to deal with.
New culture, new friends, new school, new schedule, new
classes, new language...everything feels new. We are so
consumed with our emotions and our survival that we
forget to look around at those who are experiencing the
very same feelings we are.

As I watched Wanda discuss our similarities and differences, I realized that I was becoming a mirror — something that I had never had. I couldn't help thinking of my 15-year-old self and how I longed to have had this kind of connection with someone who could inspire me to be my best. Even today, I go out of my way to find books where I can meet characters who are undocumented immigrants or otherwise similar to me because, as a little kid, I never read anything like that. So for me to be able to be that for these kids — to see these kids open up and express themselves like that after reading my story — feels like one of the most important things I could ever do.

But guess what? Your story can have an equally powerful impact on the people in your life. It doesn't matter how old you are — you have experiences that are worthy of sharing, that can help you achieve your dreams and inspire others to overcome their struggles. But your story can only be powerful if you share it and keep it alive. Whatever pain, whatever struggle you've experienced, it's not for you to forget it or to put it behind you. Don't let it keep hurting you, but use it as energy to move through life, and keep it strong because you never know when you might encounter someone who is going through the same things as you. If it's not fresh for you at that moment — if it's something you've left in the past — then how will you use your experience to inspire someone else?

Telling your stories teaches you to embrace your past and the process you went through to become who you are. Your story is your journey, like the caterpillar who goes through a difficult, unglamorous transformation in order to become a beautiful butterfly. For you to become that beautiful person who can help and impact society, you must embrace your own process — your language, your stories, your past, your ugly, your pretty, and everything you are.

That's why I encourage all of my students to write their stories down, because it makes you stop and think, "Where am I from? What have I done? What has happened to me that hurt me, that touched my heart?" Just thinking about your past so deeply can be a powerful healing process. It was for me when I sat down and wrote my story out for that newcomer class, in a very different way than when I told it to newspapers or in that very first job interview. When I sat down and wrote it out, it made me realize just how much I have overcome and how many memories I have in my heart that I had not taken the time to appreciate as I should. In a way, it felt like I was unpacking something I had kept hidden away for many years. I had started packing up my past and my experiences the year I started high school. Instead of developing my own identity and individuality during that first year in the United States, I'd felt like I had to assimilate to avoid sticking out. I betrayed my identity by packing it away.

Yet, all my memories and experiences were still alive, even after years of being abandoned and ignored. I found a sense of freedom in embracing and sharing my story — in actually being who I am instead of trying to be someone else to please others.

So now that you've read my story, I encourage you to sit down and think about your own. Think about activities you do with your cousins. Think about the favorite meal you prepare with your mom or your grandma. Think about conversations you've had with the important people in your life. These memories don't have to be big and important. When I close my eyes, the very first thing I think of is being seven years old and babysitting my sister. She loved to climb this one tree in our yard, and no matter how many times I asked her not to, she would always climb it and come down covered in dirt, so I'd have to clean her up and change her clothes before our mom came home. See? That doesn't seem like a very important memory — it's not a big event or a very exciting day — but it does tell a lot about my childhood because it shows that I was already taking care of my younger siblings at just seven years old.

Now it's your turn. Close your eyes, and think back through your experiences. What do you remember first? Something sad? Something happy? Something boring and routine? I encourage you to start writing these memories down in a journal. The letters my mom and I wrote to each other when I was in Guatemala bring back memories that I'd completely erased from my recollection of the past. The journals I kept as a teenager did the same thing. At the time, they helped me process what I was going through — from taking care of my siblings to dropping out of school to getting pregnant and everything else. I wrote about the big moments, of course, but what I treasure most are the memories of the little moments: what I missed about my mom, what I loved about school and my job at the supermarket, and the little things that frustrated or excited me.

You can write about all those things too. If your siblings are getting on your nerves, write it down. What are they doing to bother you? What do you wish they would do instead? If you're missing your best friend from back home, write that down too. What's your best memory with your friend? What do you miss most about her? What would you say to her if you were sitting next to each other right now? No thought or feeling is too unimportant to write down.

No matter how small they seem — like the Mexican jackets my sisters and I bought or the clown sticker I sent my mom — all those little moments are part of your story, and they're shaping you into the person you are and the person you will become.

Thank you for letting me share my story on these pages. I can't wait to hear yours.

Your teacher ALWAYS,
♡ Ms. Francis

Emily's Acknowledgements

I would like to begin by thanking God, who has taken me and my family with *su mano poderosa* from where we were to where we are today—with so many blessings and opportunities, including the opportunity to share my story with you all in this book.

I would also like to thank my mother, Leslie Zamara Bonilla, whose strength and support have always been an essential part of my journey. Without her encouragement, I never would have been able to become a teacher and to live the life I do today.

I have been blessed with a beautiful family. My husband, David, has believed in me and supported me every step of the way, even when we faced hard times. I'm also grateful to my children, David and Hannah, who were the fuel that ignited my decision to enter "professional" life and move from working as a cashier to becoming a classroom teacher, where I have been able to make an impact on so many lives.

Of course, I want to thank my abuelita, without whose help I never would have been able to become a citizen of this wonderful country. I must also thank my Tía Rosy and Tío Jimmy, who have been an essential part of my journey. They trusted me enough to give me a new start in North Carolina. With their help, I was able to put my life back together, get my

GED, and eventually become a teacher's aid. From there, my life was transformed under the guidance of my dear friend, teacher, and mentor Angie Power. She took me under her wing, taught me, coached me, and guided me for eight years while I was her assistant.

I can't fail to mention all the support I have received from friends I have made through my professional learning network (PLN). I especially want to thank Dr. Carol Salva, who validated my story and encouraged me to share it publicly. Her prompting inspired me to tell my story for the first time, with her students, and then with so many others who have held up my story as a mirror to their own experiences. I am so proud that my story and those of my brother, Abner, and my sisters, Leslie, Lisbeth, and Gabriela, are now a part of so many other people's stories. My siblings and their children will always mean so much to me.

Finally, I will always be extremely grateful for Sarah Welch and John Seidlitz, who guided me through the writing process. Without their help, I never would have been able to move my thoughts from my head to the page. Their support— and the support of so many people at Seidlitz Education— made this book possible.

¡Gracias a todos!

Hola!

My name is Astrid Emily Francis, I was born in Guatemala and came to the U.S.A. at the age of 15. I am married to a wonderful and supporting man, David. I have two wonderful children, David and Hannah. I am the oldest of five children (I have three sisters and a brother). I adore my mother Leslie, whose strength is the reason I am able to live my dream.

I teach at Concord High School in Concord, North Carolina. In this role I serve students serve students throughout all four grade levels at various English proficiency levels. My experience as an English language learner inspired me to become an ESL teacher. I have a deep understanding of the challenges my students must overcome in order to find success. I go above and beyond my teaching responsibilities to build a school-community relationship in support of student learning.

I earned a BA in Spanish and an MAT in Teaching ESL from UNC-Charlotte. I've served as a professional development facilitator, motivational speaker for newly hired teachers, keynote speaker, ESL PLC lead, teacher liaison for Cabarrus County Board of Education, Teacher of the Year 2016, co-operating teacher, and mentor to beginning ESL teachers. I am also a board member of the Carolina TESOL.

As a leader, my motto and focus is to INSPIRE students to dream more, learn more, do more, and become more!